# Introduct[ion]

This book of fifteen walking tours is a [...] city, that area between the Grand Canal on the south side of the Liffey and the Royal Canal on the north side of the river.

Some of the tours are relatively short (1-1½ hours), however the majority range between 1½-3 hours. Each tour can be completed in a morning or an afternoon. If you are not in a rush, the longer tours can quite easily be stretched out over an entire day, stopping for lunch along the way.

Throughout the text, numbered square brackets direct you to a page in the book with more information on the place you are reading about. Sometimes, this may only be a sentence or two, while in other cases the page to which you have been directed may contain more detailed information.

I have tried to include as many places of interest as possible. However, on occasion, I was forced to omit a house or park or local amenity simply because the journey there and back would have made the walk too long. The omissions are minor when compared to what has been included.

While the book is primarily a homage to a great city, it does not shy away from criticising where I felt criticism was due. Most cities in Britain and in Ireland have suffered from some appalling planning decisions – or lack of them – over the past forty years. Dublin is no exception. Right up to present times, much building development and road construction in the capital has resulted in a diminution of the city's architectural heritage. In many cases, where old buildings could have been saved and restored, too often the easy demolition-and-build-new option was chosen. Sadly, a recurring urban theme of the last forty years has been the lack of an overall visual plan for the city.

That said, this book set out to celebrate one of Europe's great cities and I believe it does that. Dublin is a joy to walk around and there is rarely a dull moment on all fifteen tours. The key to getting the most out of the walks is: take your time, look around, rest and reflect – you will be less tired at the end of each walk than if you attempt to complete each tour in as short a time as possible. Happy strolling!

# Acknowledgments

My thanks to family and friends who gave of their time, energy and shoe leather. Each one of the fifteen walks is a better all round tour as a direct result of their constructive suggestions and criticisms.

My thanks also to Fergal Tobin of Gill & Macmillan who displayed rare lack of judgment in agreeing to pay me for doing what I like best – walking around my native city.

My thanks to my normally intelligent brother who displayed an unaccustomed masochistic streak in offering to read the entire manuscript before I handed it over to my publishers. I am grateful to him for biting his lip and not telling me to start all over again.

Finally, my thanks in advance to each and every stroller who follows one or more or even all of the tours in this book. I hope you enjoy the strolling as much as I enjoyed the planning, researching and writing.

This edition published by Passport Books
A division of NTC/Contemporary Publishing Group, Inc.
4255 West Touhy Avenue, Lincolnwood (Chicago), IL 60646–1975
U.S.A.

© Gerry Boland 1999

Published in conjunction with
Gill & Macmillan
Goldenbridge, Dublin 8

Produced by Language & Publishing Partners International
65 Abberley, Shanganagh Road, Killiney, Co. Dublin
Printed by: Edelvives, Spain

International Standard Book Number: 0–658–00076–4
Library of Congress Catalog Card Number: on file

All maps are based on the Ordnance Survey
by permission of the Government (permit no. 6842)

# Contents

Grafton Street, Dublin's most popular thoroughfare, possesses an interesting history and boasts a graceful, largely nineteenth-century street line. Yet it is somehow its atmosphere, at once convivial and local, drifting through the street's gentle curves, which ultimately defines it. And it *is* curious that the atmosphere is local, for the street attracts today almost as many international visitors as native Dubliners.

At just over one mile, and lasting a leisurely one hour, this tour is the shortest in the book. It can be undertaken at any time of the day or night, as there are always people around. For any first time visitor to the city, it is a tour which simply cannot be missed.

## Tour Facts
- **Length of tour:**
  1.2 miles (1.9 kilometres)
- **Duration of tour:**
  a leisurely hour
- **Refreshments:**
  wherever takes your fancy, the choice is wide and varied
- **Getting to the Starting Point:**
  if you don't know where Trinity College is, ask any passerby
- **Special Note for Walkers:**
  most of the shops and department stores close between 5.30pm and 6pm, Monday to Saturday. Late opening till 9pm on Thursday. Some shops open on Sunday.

## Opening Times
- **Dublin Civic Museum**
  Telephone (01) 679 4260
  Tues–Sat 10am–6pm
  Sunday 11am–2pm
  Closed Monday
- **Powerscourt Townhouse Centre**
  Telephone (01) 679 4144
  Mon–Sat 9am–6pm
  (7pm on Thursday)

**Tour begins:** *at the front gates of Trinity College.*

Trinity College is explored in some of the other tours in this book, in particular *Southside Georgian* [**52**]. Across College Green to your right is the Bank of Ireland, built as the Irish Parliament in 1729 [**53**]. Directly ahead is Dame Street, which leads to Dublin Castle and the cathedrals of Christ Church and St Patrick.

Turn left outside the gates and walk along the lower part of Grafton Street. Across the street are some fine, late nineteenth and early twentieth-century buildings, most notably that which houses the Trustee Savings Bank at number 114. On this left side is the main entrance to the **Provost's House**, built in 1759 and believed to be from an original design by Palladio. Three almost identical houses were built around the same time: in Old Burlington Street, London in

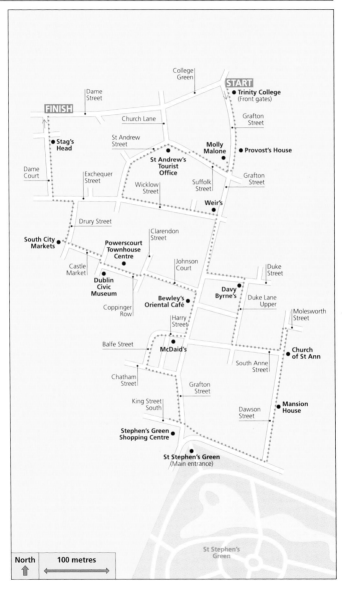

START
● Trinity College
(Front gates)

Grafton
Street

College
Green

Dame
Street

FINISH

Church Lane

St Andrew
Street

● Stag's
Head

Molly
Malone

● Provost's House

Dame
Court

Exchequer
Street

St Andrew's
Tourist
Office

Grafton
Street

Wicklow
Street

Suffolk
Street

● Weir's

Drury Street

South City
Markets ●

Clarendon
Street

Powerscourt
Townhouse
Centre

Castle
Market

Johnson
Court

Duke
Street

Dublin
Civic
Museum

Bewley's
Oriental Café ●

Davy
Byrne's

Duke Lane
Upper

Coppinger
Row

Harry
Street

Molesworth
Street

Balfe Street

McDaid's ●

● Church
of St Ann

South Anne
Street

Chatham
Street

Grafton
Street

King Street
South

Dawson
Street

● Mansion
House

Stephen's Green
Shopping Centre ●

St Stephen's Green
(Main entrance)

St Stephen's
Green

North
↑

100 metres
⟵⟶

**5**

Molly selling her wares

Nonetheless, as a piece of popular street sculpture, it has made its mark. Molly was a street trader who was immortalised by the song in which she 'wheeled her wheelbarrow through streets broad and narrow, crying cockles and mussels alive-alive-o!' As a young boy growing up in the city, I was led to believe that Molly had been a waif-like figure, living in poverty and clad in rags as she went about her daily business. Jeanne Rynhart's sculpture suggests otherwise and leaves the onlooker wondering if it was cockles and mussels she was selling, or some sort of comfort that had nothing at all to do with food!

Walk a few steps from Molly towards Grafton Street and stop to look left along Nassau Street, originally named St Patrick's Well Lane. The fine wrought iron railings running the length of the street form the southern perimeter of Trinity College and were erected in 1842. The street itself was raised by about three metres, the material mainly coming from the area around the Viking *Thingmote*, the site of which you will pass in a few moments.

Turn right and walk along Suffolk Street. Among the many cafés and restaurants here is Tosca, on the left, the proprietor of which is the brother of U2's lead singer, Bono. At the end of the street on the right is one of Dublin's more interesting pubs, **O'Neill's [146]**. The pub has a lovely, rounded Victorian façade and a fine clock between the doors. Inside, there are five individual bars or lounges, each

1723, in Potsdam in 1755 for Frederick the Great, and the Trinity College Provost's House. This is the only survivor. Provosts of Trinity College have lived here since 1759. The house is private.

Thirty metres beyond the Provost's House, cross to the right at the pedestrian lights and have a look at the **Molly Malone** statue, erected in 1988 as one of the many pieces of street sculpture commissioned to commemorate Dublin's Millennium. It is a popular attraction for visitors to the city, but most Dubliners I know either do not like it or choose to ignore its existence. Within artistic circles, it has few admirers and many detractors.

one of them hard to find a seat in at most times of the day.

Cross, exercising caution on account of the heavy traffic, to the converted Protestant **Church of St Andrew [66]**. The building is now the principal drop-in tourist information centre in the city and stands on the approximate site of the Thingmote, a forty-foot mound on which the Vikings held their parliament and overlooked activities down on Hoggen (now College) Green, where you started the tour.

Continue past the old church. Across the street is St Andrew Street Post Office, recently revamped to enable it accommodate the large number of foreign visitors who use its services. Further along is ENFO, where you can pick up a wide range of information on the state of Ireland's environment. There are regular exhibitions on the ground floor which can be informative. Proceed, past the numerous restaurants on either side, and stop at the corner of St Andrew Street and Wicklow Street. Beside you is one of the city's finest old bars, the **International [146]**. Across the street is the Old Stand, named after a now-demolished spectator stand in Lansdowne Road rugby stadium. No prizes for guessing, then, that this pub is a magnet for rugby supporters on international rugby weekends. Turn left into Wicklow Street and rejoin Grafton Street after a couple of hundred metres.

On the corner is one of Dublin's landmark shops, **Weir's Jewellers and Silversmiths**.

Records show that the Weir story began in Scotland in or about 1862, when James Weir opened for business in Argyle Street, in central Glasgow, as a watchmaker. Three years later, his son Thomas Weir left Glasgow and travelled to Dublin to establish himself as a jeweller in Ireland. In 1869, he started his own modest enterprise in the centre of his adopted city. Little did he know that, 130 years later, the premises bearing his name would have outlasted almost every other retail premises on the street. The site on which Weir's stands today was previously occupied by some humble, traditional-style establishments. At number 1 Wicklow Street, John Fulham had a small tobacconist's shop, while at number 2, Richard Mallett owned the Fox Tavern. At number 3, Alexander Ogilvy ran a silk mercer's shop. Weir's current chairman, David Andrews, is a great-grandson of the founder Thomas Weir, and is the only direct descendant now working in the jewellers.

Look left and right along **Grafton Street**. In 1869, when Weir's was establishing itself here, the street was very different to the bustling thoroughfare of today. Then, it was a street for leisurely strolls by the well-off gentlefolk of Dublin; occasionally, a horse-drawn hansom cab would pass by, the sound of the horses' hooves echoing on the cobblestones.

Further back in time, the street was a medieval laneway leading from Hoggen Green to the marshy and wild open space Dubliners

A bad hair day on Grafton Street

and none too soon – the clutter and chaos forced the city authorities to take action and, in 1982, the street was pedestrianised, changing it overnight into a sane and hospitable oasis in the heart of the city. The only downside to all this is that very few of the original shops have survived – the astronomical rents having pushed all but the most stoic of survivors either out of business or off the street to less aggressively commercial locations.

Across from Weir's is **Brown Thomas**, once Dublin's finest department store but now not quite so splendid or unique on account of its regrettable move a couple of years back from its original and atmospheric home where Marks and Spencer now stands across the street. One has to admit that M&S did an impressive job of building a new store in the manner of the old Brown Thomas, but nothing could ever quite be like the olde-world character and feel of the original Brown Thomas, a store established in 1848 by John Brown and James Thomas.

As you stroll up the street, look up at the fine buildings which sometimes are forgotten about, amidst the frenzied shopping sprees. Take the first left into Duke Street, named in 1723 after the second Duke of Grafton, son of Charles II, who also provided the name for Grafton Street itself. A famous literary landmark here is **Davy Byrne's** pub, on the right [**149**]. Every Bloomsday (16 June) hundreds of Joycean scholars and a diverse assortment

know and love today as St Stephen's Green. In the 1790s, the city's axis shifted with the development of Sackville (now O'Connell) Street, Carlisle (now O'Connell) Bridge and Westmoreland and D'Olier Streets. Grafton Street began to lose its tranquil, residential air, adopting in its place a commercial character. By the eighteenth century it had become popular among booksellers and publishers and many belonging to these trades lived on the street.

During the nineteenth and twentieth centuries, the street became more and more commercial (though relatively tranquil in comparison to today) and, by the 1960s, it was a noisy, bustling street, filled with shoppers, traders, buses, lorries, cars and bicycles. Eventually –

of Joycean characters assemble around the pub at lunchtime, the time of day during which the main character in *Ulysses*, Leopold Bloom, pays a visit.

Across the street is another pub, The Bailey, which has been rebuilt in recent times and has lost something in the process – character, I think it's called! In the pub's hallway stood for many years the Georgian door of number 7 Eccles Street, off Dorset Street, where Leopold Bloom lived or, rather, where Joyce fictionally placed him. The Eccles Street house was demolished in the 1960s. The famous door can now be seen in the James Joyce Cultural Institute on North Great George's Street [**119**]. Further along Duke Street on the left is **The Duke** (formerly *Larry Tobin's* and once a place full of character – and characters), renovated a couple of years back and losing all its old charm in the process.

Go right, into the narrow pedestrianised street running beside Davy Byrne's. This leads into the **Royal Hibernian Way Shopping Mall**, built on the site of the Royal Hibernian Hotel. Continue to **Kehoe's** pub [**149**] on the right, one of Dublin's most authentic pubs and an unusual survivor in a city gone mad with pub renovation ('renovation' in this context being a misnomer for 'ripping the character out of them').

Turn left into South Anne Street. Directly ahead is the very fine Anglican **Church of St Ann**, built in 1729 and retaining much of Isaac Wills' eighteenth-century interior. Extensive renovations carried out by Thomas Deane in 1868 changed the church's original exterior, but it remains an impressive sight and provides a very pleasing perspective down South Anne Street.

Turn left into Dawson Street and cross to the far side at the pedestrian lights ten metres down. Directly ahead is Molesworth Street at the end of which you can see **Leinster House**, home of Dáil Éireann, the Irish Parliament [**48**]. Do not go down here – you can visit it later, if you like.

Turn right and walk past **St Ann's Church**, taking time out to explore the interior, if it is open. The church hosts regular classical recitals, so check if there are any lunchtime concerts coming up. Near the altar, there is a shelf which dates to 1723 and recalls an unusual bequest by the Right Hon. Theophilus Lord Newton that loaves of bread be left there every day for the poor people of Dublin, a tradition which lasts to the present day.

A few doors along, at number 19, is the **Royal Irish Academy**, founded in 1785 by the Royal Dublin Society. The house was designed by John Ensor in 1769 and has been home to the Academy since 1852. The RIA holds a major collection of Irish manuscripts and publishes papers on archaeology, history, literature and science. Directly across the street and in complete contrast is one of the city's yuppiest bars, the **Café en Seine** [**150**].

Beside the Royal Irish Academy is the **Mansion House**, built in a Queen Anne style in

1710 for Joshua Dawson who became bankrupt soon after. The house was subsequently sold in 1715 for £3,500 to Dublin Corporation and has been used as the official residence of the Lord Mayor of Dublin ever since. The original building was in brick, but the façade was altered in 1851, with the cast-iron porch being added in 1886. Much of the interior has also been altered over the years, though it remains quite a sumptuous residence. The Lord Mayor is elected by Dublin City Council on or around the fourth of July for a one-year term of office. The Round Room, behind the main house, was designed by Francis Johnston and built in 1821, specifically for the visit of King George IV. On 21 January 1919, the first Irish Parliament, unrecognised by the British Government, adopted the Declaration of Independence in this building. Unfortunately, neither the Mansion House proper, nor its adjoining Round Room, is open to the casual (forgive the presumption) visitor.

Across the street is a façade from a bygone age. The building belongs to the **Royal Irish Automobile Club (RIAC)** and the wood-panelled façade at ground-floor level is rarely seen in Dublin these days. Further along the same side is a narrow entrance to 'Dublin's Smallest Pub', the **Dawson Lounge**. Try it for size!

At the top of the street, turn right and walk along the right side of St Stephen's Green, passing as you go an impressive line of Georgian houses, many now occupied by commercial outlets. The large houses of numbers 8 and 9 are particularly interesting. Both were Victorian clubs with an exclusively male membership, and they remain male clubs. Number 9, just beyond the Aer Lingus building, was built in the 1750s and houses the **St Stephen's Green Club**. The interior contains fine rococo plasterwork by the celebrated Francini brothers. Further along, at number 8, with its curved steps and balustrades, is the **Hibernian United Services Club**. The house was built in the 1770s for the Bishop of Killala and contains some fine plasterwork. Sir Walter Scott stayed overnight in 1825.

Stop at the top of Grafton Street and get your bearings. Across to your left is the Fusiliers' Arch, the main entrance to **St Stephen's Green**. The 'Green' is extensively covered in the *Three City Parks* tour. Beside you is the **Stephen's Green Shopping Centre**, a massive (in Dublin terms) commercial development, built in 1989, with dozens of small and medium-sized shops, cafés and two large department stores. The exterior, which is over-elaborate and inappropriate to its location, is already showing telltale signs of deterioration. This is a pity, because the airy and bright interior is very impressive, if a little cluttered at the entrance.

Running along the side of the shopping centre is South King Street. A brief detour will bring you to the **Gaiety**, an olde-world theatre well known for its staging of musicals and popular shows. It

Strollers on Grafton Street

was designed by C.J. Phipps, a leading Victorian theatre architect. It opened its doors in 1871 and is Dublin's oldest extant theatre.

Retrace your steps and go left into Grafton Street. From here, you can enjoy the gentle curve of the street, so unlike the straight lines of much of the classical city. Just before the first street on the left, you will see the narrowest of passages. This is called Tangier Lane and leads, on the left side, into the stage door of the Gaiety and, on the right side, into the lounge of Neary's pub. As you might imagine, a much-travelled path between the two over the years!

Turn left into Chatham Street, named after William Pitt, first Earl of Chatham. **The Chatham Lounge [148]**, known by locals as *Neary's*, is worth a look, not least for its fine façade. Take the second right into **Balfe Street**,

named after Michael William Balfe, composer of *The Bohemian Girl*, who was born here in 1808. At the bottom of the street is the luxurious Westbury Hotel and the adjoining Westbury Shopping Mall. Go right and into Harry Street.

On your right is **McDaid's [148]**, a legendary pub in terms of its literary significance. It was frequented by that ofttimes troublesome trio of writers, Brendan Behan [108], Patrick Kavanagh [103] and Brian O'Nolan (Flann O'Brien) [109]. Opposite McDaid's is **Bruxelles**, a pub with a fine Victorian façade and turret, built in 1890 to the design of J.J. O'Callaghan, one of Dublin's most prolific pub architects of the day.

Go past both pubs and rejoin Grafton Street, turning left and strolling to **Bewley's Oriental Café** on the left, Dublin's most

**11**

famous coffee house. The company was founded in the early 1840s by a Quaker, Joshua Bewley, a tea merchant and the youngest son of Samuel Bewley. Samuel was a successful silk merchant and descendant of Mungo Bewley, the first of the Bewleys to arrive in Ireland from England, as far back as 1700. In 1894, the company opened its first Oriental Café, in South Great George's Street. Two years later, a café was opened in Westmoreland Street and, in 1927, the Grafton Street branch was opened. All three still thrive.

Bewley's has always been one of the city's great meeting points and we can take it for granted that many of Dublin's most famous and infamous characters sat drinking tea or coffee here; we know that James Joyce discussed his idea to open up a cinema (the Volta on Dublin's Mary Street) here, and that the poet Patrick

Kavanagh was a frequent visitor. A look inside, then, is essential, not least to admire the splendid stained glass windows by Harry Clarke at ground-floor level. However, this may not be as easy as it sounds. A recent and major development did away with the previously casual, chaotic yet agreeable and convivial self-service ground-floor café, and replaced it with a polished, table-service arrangement which limits the casual access enjoyed by so many natives and visitors alike for so long. For many of the die-hard Bewley's fans, it was the end of an era.

**Whyte's Academy** (1758-1824), a boys' school of solid repute, once stood on the site of Bewley's. It was founded by Samuel Whyte and assisted in the education of the playwright Richard Brinsley Sheridan, the poet Thomas Moore, the republican Robert Emmet, and

Mansion House at night

Arthur Wellesley, later to become the Duke of Wellington. The Duke's father, Lord Mornington, lived in Grafton Street until 1765, when he moved to Upper Merrion Street.

Running along the side of Bewley's is a narrow laneway, Johnson Court. The Catholic **St Teresa's Church**, also known as the Carmelite Friary, is hidden away on the right of the laneway, in the unobtrusive manner common to many Catholic churches built during the Penal times. The friary was founded by the Discalced Carmelites in 1793 ('discalced' meaning 'barefooted or only sandalled'). For those interested in religious sculpture, a visit to view the impressive 'Dead Christ' (1829) by John Hogan, located beneath the high altar, is imperative.

Continue along the laneway. Directly ahead is the **Powerscourt Townhouse Centre**, a splendid, eighteenth-century Georgian townhouse, converted in the 1970s to an attractive indoor shopping mall. Do not enter from this side, but instead go left and immediately right into Coppinger Row. On the left corner, at the end of this pedestrian street, is the **Dublin Civic Museum**, which houses an interesting collection of artifacts relating to the city.

Cross to Grogan's pub and turn around and look at the front of **Powerscourt Townhouse [45]**, built for Lord Powerscourt in 1774. During shopping hours, the entire building is open to the public and it is well worth a brief diversion up the granite steps to admire some of the superbly decorated eighteenth-century rooms.

Directly opposite the townhouse is the pedestrianised Castle Market, with the very chic Cooke's Café (actually, it's a restaurant, but it's obviously even more chic to call it a café!) adding considerable style to the street. Walk to the end of Castle Market and cross to explore the covered **South City Markets** ahead. The splendid red-brick Victorian block around which the markets are centred were rebuilt in 1892 following a fire which destroyed much of the original 1881 buildings.

Exit the markets by the way you entered and turn left and walk to Exchequer Street. A right turn will bring you to the Old Stand and The International but, to finish the tour, go left and take the first right before the Central Hotel into Dame Court. The ultra-trendy [Rí-Rá] nightclub is on the left, as is the popular Odessa Restaurant. Across the street on the corner is one of Dublin's most ornate Victorian pubs, the **Stag's Head [146]**. Go through the covered passageway directly ahead to Dame Street to finish the tour.

There are so many possibilities for post-tour refreshments around here that it's difficult to know where to start. You could retrace your steps to the Stag's Head, drop in to the bar of the adjoining Mercantile Hotel, or be more adventurous and cross Dame Street and enter Temple Bar where you will have an abundant choice of pubs, cafés and restaurants.

# Around O'Connell Street

At approximately forty-five metres, O'Connell Street is Dublin's widest street. It is also its grandest. The tree-lined pedestrian mall running along its centre recalls some of the great boulevards of Paris. No other Dublin street resides in the same illustrious league.

At its centre, the building which most embodies Ireland's nationhood, the General Post Office (GPO), asserts its influence over the entire street through its bold, free-standing columns reaching out to the edge of the pavement.

The tour branches off from time to time to explore nearby places of interest, among them the Abbey Theatre and the Catholic Pro-Cathedral.

Sunday morning is an ideal time to do the tour, as traffic is light and the pavements are relatively bare. Avoid Friday and Saturday nights.

**Tour begins:** *outside Bewley's Oriental Café on Westmoreland Street.*

**Bewley's** opened here for business in 1896, thirty-one years before its most famous branch, on Grafton Street, opened [11]. It is one of the city's most popular meeting places.

Across the street is the unusual façade of the **Educational Building Society**, a completely revamped Victorian building, with glass and stone curtain walls framing the original Victorian façade. It was completed in 1976.

Walk towards O'Connell Bridge and cross at the traffic lights to the pedestrian island on the right on which various bronze footprints are embedded. This unusual street sculpture formed part of the Dublin Millennium Sculpture Symposium (1988) which brought Dublin street sculpture back into vogue, though some would argue (justifiably, in my view), that much of modern Dublin street

**Tour Facts**

- **Length of tour:** 2.2 miles (3.5 kilometres)
- **Duration of tour:** a leisurely $1\frac{1}{4}$ hours
- **Refreshments:** during the tour (the Gresham Hotel); after the tour (Bewley's Café on Westmoreland Street; Palace Bar on Fleet Street)
- **Getting to the Starting Point:** from O'Connell Bridge (walk south, towards Trinity College along the right side of Westmoreland Street. Bewley's Oriental Café is on your right); from Trinity College front gates (turn right outside the gates and walk for a hundred metres and cross to the pedestrian island and cross again to the left to the House of Lords entrance to the Bank of Ireland. Turn right and walk along Westmoreland Street. Bewley's is on your left)

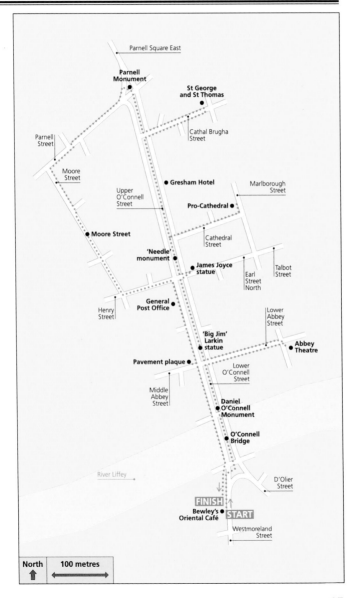

Parnell Square East

Parnell Monument

St George and St Thomas

Cathal Brugha Street

Parnell Street

Moore Street

Upper O'Connell Street

Gresham Hotel

Marlborough Street

Pro-Cathedral

Moore Street

Cathedral Street

'Needle' monument

James Joyce statue

Earl Street North

Talbot Street

General Post Office

Henry Street

'Big Jim' Larkin statue

Lower Abbey Street

Abbey Theatre

Pavement plaque

Lower O'Connell Street

Middle Abbey Street

Daniel O'Connell Monument

O'Connell Bridge

River Liffey

D'Olier Street

FINISH

Bewley's Oriental Café

START

Westmoreland Street

North

100 metres

sculpture leaves a lot to be desired. The series of sculptures at your feet is called *People's Island* and is the work of Rachel Joynt.

Stand at the centre of the island and face towards Westmoreland Street and the fine view of the House of Lords entrance to the Bank of Ireland. Immediately in front of you is the **Irish Civil Service (ICS)** building, built in 1895 for the London and Lancashire Insurance Company to a design by the well-known architect of the day, J.J. O'Callaghan. The building was nicknamed at the time O'Callaghan's Chance, suggesting that its architect was deemed to be lucky to have had his design set in such a prominent location.

Running along the left of the ICS building is D'Olier Street, one of the thoroughfares created by the Wide Streets Commission towards the end of the eighteenth century (Westmoreland Street was another).

Cross to the central island on **O'Connell Bridge** and stop beside the central lamp standard. This is one of the most dramatic locations in Dublin. Before a bridge was built here in 1794, the most easterly bridge across the Liffey was Essex (now Grattan) Bridge, spanning the river several hundred metres upriver from here. All traffic from the north side of the city destined for the Parliament on College Green would have used Essex Bridge. When O'Connell Bridge was built (it was named Sackville Bridge at that time), the axis of the city shifted eastwards, as it has been doing, albeit very slowly, since the

late Middle Ages. The original bridge was designed by the celebrated architect of the period, James Gandon. Gandon's bridge was widened and altered beyond recognition by the Dublin Port and Docks Board in 1880, trebling its original width.

From here, look left and up the River Liffey quays. The pedestrian **Halfpenny Bridge** [33] is probably the city's most photographed bridge. In the distance, you can easily pick out the slender spire of the church of **St Augustine and St John** on Thomas Street and, to its right, the spire of **Christ Church Cathedral**. Still looking upriver, along the right (north) quay, you can see in the foreground a line of interesting quayside buildings running west from O'Connell Bridge. Some of these buildings are a couple of hundred years old but many are relatively new imitations. The Liffey Quays were once regarded as essential to the character of the city, but a combination of neglect and unimaginative development – more in evidence the further one travels up the quays – has diminished this character considerably.

Turn around and look downstream, towards where the river meets the Irish Sea at the Liffey's mouth. The high-rise building is **Liberty Hall**, now an accepted resident of the city's skyline but unlikely to win any friends for its design. It was built in 1966 and is the home of the Irish trade unions. The rest of the view east is interrupted by the crude Loop Line railway bridge.

Numerous proposals over the years to reduce its negative visual impact or to move the line over the river to another location have come to nought. Beyond this bridge is the **Custom House [54]**, designed by James Gandon and widely regarded as Dublin's finest Georgian public building.

Where you are standing is the pulse of the city. At four in the morning, when normal souls are long since tucked inside their warm beds, life in a diversity of forms goes benignly – and sometimes not so benignly – about its dusky business. Stray commuters commute, lost souls flutter by, drunks lurch against the bridge-stone as they stagger somewhere, anywhere, God-knows-where. A lone Garda observes dispassionately the restless forms of human life which enter and leave his line of vision. It is not a time to be out and, I presume, you are not. If you are, leave this tour immediately and go home to your bed. This is not a tour to be done at the bewitching hour!

Cross to the central mall on O'Connell Street proper. The monument ahead commemorates the life and work of 'the Liberator' **Daniel O'Connell** (1775-1847). O'Connell was the key political figure in Ireland in the early part of the 1800s. His two principal political obsessions were the repeal of the Act of Union (with Great Britain) and Catholic Emancipation. A passionate believer in non-violence throughout his political life, he fought peacefully and ultimately effectively to achieve

O'Connell Monument

these goals for the Irish people. The **O'Connell Monument** was begun in 1864 and unveiled in 1882. It is the work of sculptor John Henry Foley and comprises a 3.6 m bronze figure of O'Connell, standing above about thirty figures, representing various strata of Irish society: members of the church, the professions, the arts and the working classes. The central, female figure of Erin, facing the river, is holding in her hand a copy of the Catholic Emancipation Act of 1829. Beneath these figures are four seated, winged figures. They represent Fidelity (with an Irish Wolfhound), Courage (with a serpent), Eloquence (holding a book), and Patriotism (with a sword and shield).

Remain on the central mall, lined with plane trees, and walk the length of the street. *[There will be diversions left and right as you proceed.]* At the first junction is a monument to **William Smith**

**17**

**O'Brien** (1803-64), arms folded, holding a scroll. The inscription tells us that he was sentenced to death for high treason during the Rising of 1848. He served five years in Tasmania and was eventually given an unconditional release, whereupon he returned to Ireland but remained politically inactive until his death.

A brief diversion down the street to your right, Lower Abbey Street, will bring you past the traditional and recently restored Wynn's Hotel to the **Abbey Theatre**, on the corner with Marlborough Street a couple of hundred metres from O'Connell Street. The Abbey was founded by Lady Gregory and William Butler Yeats and opened in 1904. It had a turbulent beginning, one of its earliest staged plays being John Millington Synge's *The Playboy of the Western World*, during which rioting broke out among a puritanical audience shocked by what they saw as the play's immoral tone. Riots again erupted in 1926 when Seán O'Casey's *The Plough and the Stars* fuelled the nationalist ire of the audience by its honest attempt to portray the drama of the Easter Rising. In 1951, the building was destroyed by fire and, in 1966, the present building, designed by Michael Scott, was opened. For Ireland's national theatre, its façade is depressingly uninspired.

Cross to the **Flowing Tide** pub [**145**] and go left and return to O'Connell Street. Cross to the central mall. Beside you is a monument in white Italian marble to **Sir John Gray** (1815-75), proprietor of the Freeman's

Journal newspaper and MP for Kilkenny City. Gray was a Protestant nationalist and supported the Repeal movement led by O'Connell. He is commemorated here, however, for an entirely different reason. As chairman of the Dublin Corporation Waterworks Committee, he was instrumental in bringing the Vartry Water Supply to the city and suburbs in the 1860s, a major contribution to the development of the city at the time.

Continue along the mall. **Eason's** on your left was founded in 1919 and has sold books, newspapers and magazines to millions of Dubliners over the years. The dramatic figure ahead, with outstretched arms, is Oisín Kelly's heroic statue of **'Big Jim' Larkin**. The pose, in full oratorical flight, symbolises the passion and power of the inspirational trade union leader who pioneered the trade union movement in Ireland, founding in 1909 the Irish Transport and General Workers' Union (ITGWU) and, in 1924, the Workers' Union of Ireland. The ITGWU represented largely the unskilled workers of Dublin – dockers, labourers, factory hands – workers whose living conditions in some of the worst slums in Europe were truly appalling. The bitter 'Lockout Strike' of 1913 was caused when employers demanded of their workers that they sign a statement guaranteeing they would not join Larkin's union. The city came to a virtual standstill for much of the duration of the strike, which lasted from

August 1913 until February 1914.

Larkin died on 30 January 1947 and he is movingly remembered here by Monaghan poet Patrick Kavanagh and Dublin dramatist Seán O'Casey. On another side of the plinth are the immortal words of Larkin: 'The great appear great because we are on our knees. Let us rise.'

The Larkin monument is directly opposite one of Dublin's best known department stores, **Clery's**, founded in 1941 on the site of the New Palatial Mart, built in 1852 and a predecessor of the modern department store. Between the closure of the New Palatial Mart and the Easter Rising of 1916, the building housed the Imperial Hotel. It was from one of the hotel balconies that Larkin gave a rousing speech to the 1913 strikers below, after which about four hundred people were injured during repeated baton charges. Architecturally, the building is unremarkable; however, the fine stone carvings, fluted columns and the array of clam and oyster shells on its façade give the building a lift.

Across the street is the imposing **General Post Office**, built to the design of Francis Johnston between 1814 and 1818. It is the principal post office for Dublin City and is open seven days a week. The three statues on top of the building were sculpted by Edward Smyth and represent Hibernia, with spear and harp; Mercury, holding a purse; and Fidelity, holding a key. The Ionic portico is faced with Portland stone and the rest of the building is made from granite.

The GPO was the principal location of the 1916 Easter Rising; the events which took place during the week the building was occupied by members of the Irish Citizen Army and Irish Volunteers changed the course of Irish history. Following its virtual destruction during both the 1916 Rising and the 1922 Civil War, the building remained closed until 1929. A bronze memorial to the Easter Rising inside the central, ground-floor window, sculpted by Oliver Sheppard, is a representation of the mythic Cuchulainn, dying, with a raven on his shoulder. The words of the Proclamation of 1916, read out on the street on the morning of the Rising by Patrick Pearse, are imprinted on the statue's plinth, as are the names of its signatories.

Beside the GPO and running at right angles to O'Connell Street is the city's busiest shopping thoroughfare, **Henry Street**, named after the Earl of Drogheda, Henry Moore. The same Henry Moore left his mark on this area as follows: Henry Street, Moore Street, Earl Street, Of Lane (no, that's not a joke!) and Drogheda (now O'Connell) Street. Of Lane is no longer with us, but Henry, Moore and Earl are thriving streets adjoining O'Connell Street.

Stand on the central mall with your back to Henry Street and look east, down **North Earl Street**. The building in the distance facing you is Connolly Station, one of Dublin's mainline train stations, named after James Connolly, one of the leaders of the 1916 Rising. Cross and have a look at the bronze statue ten metres down North Earl Street, beside the Kylemore Café, of **James Joyce [111]**, sculpted by Marjorie Fitzgibbon and unveiled by the Lord Mayor of Dublin on 16 June 1990. Return to the central mall at the spot where you left it. From this point to its northern end, O'Connell Street was, in the 1720s, Drogheda Street – a narrow lane which led from a country road (now Parnell Street) to where the GPO stands today. The Georgian developer, Luke Gardiner, acquired Henry Moore's estate and proceeded to turn Drogheda Street into the residential and sublime Gardiner's Mall in the late 1740s. During the latter half of that century, when its name had changed to Sackville Street, it was regarded as one of the most prestigious addresses in the city. At one stage, about ten peers and a dozen MPs had addresses here. From where you are standing to the Liffey, a warren of narrow streets had built up over the preceeding years. Following the construction of Carlisle (now O'Connell) Bridge in 1794, these streets were demolished and Sackville Street was extended to the Liffey, finally settling on its present name, O'Connell Street, in 1924.

Continue along the central mall for twenty metres until you reach the **Anna Livia Fountain**, erected during Dublin's Millennium year celebrations in 1988. The controversial sculpture is more commonly – and irreverently – referred to as *the floozie in the jacuzzi*, and in a strange way has achieved some sort of notoriety as a result, though not the kind the

sculptor had hoped for, I suspect. It sits on the site of Nelson Pillar, the graceful Doric column, erected in 1808 as a memorial to Admiral Nelson and which majestically overlooked the street until its violent demise in 1966. Apart from it being none too pleasing on the eye, it unfortunately (though this is not the sculpture's fault) acts as a rubbish magnet for every litter lout who passes by or sits on its edge. When the water is flowing, plastic bottles and fast-food containers bob up and down in a comic dance. Plans to erect a dramatic needle-like sculpture on this site are well advanced.

On a more positive and visually pleasing note, look over at the fine Victorian National Irish Bank building across from the fountain, before continuing along the mall. As you proceed, take a look at one of the iron lamp standards which line the mall. The three castles at the bottom and the city's motto – *obedientia, felicitas, civium urbis* – can be seen throughout the city on miscellaneous street furniture and on public buildings. The motto translates as 'Happy the city where citizens obey'.

At the public toilets, divert to the right down **Cathedral Street** (take care crossing as there are no pedestrian lights at this point). The narrow street leads to the Church of St Mary, more commonly referred to as the **Pro-Cathedral**. This fine Greek Doric cathedral, built between 1815 and 1825 to a design by a relatively unknown architect and exiled United Irishman, John Sweetman, would not be out of place on O'Connell Street. Indeed, it was on

## A guide to the alternative names for Dublin's street sculptures

An unusual feature (some might cynically argue *the* only redeeming feature) of some of Dublin's best-known, modern street sculptures are the names Dublin wits have coined for the statues. Joyce, with his cane, on North Earl Street, is privately (for obvious reasons) referred to as *the prick with the stick*. Others nicknamed are the Anna Livia Fountain on O'Connell Street (*the floozie in the jacuzzi* or *the hoor in the sewer*); Molly Malone on Grafton Street (*the tart with the cart*); Meeting Place on Lower Liffey Street (*the hags with the bags*); Oscar Wilde in Merrion Square (*the fag on the crag*); the floating clock in the Liffey, beneath O'Connell Bridge, which was meant to count down the seconds to the Millennium but which became unreadable and has since been removed (*the chime in the slime*)

O'Connell Street that the cathedral was originally to be located. However, although a site was available where the GPO now stands, the Catholic authorities decided in their wisdom not to offend their Protestant brethren and built their cathedral safely out of harm's way.

Across the road (Marlborough Street) to the right, behind the railings and shielded by the trees, is **Tyrone House**, a 1740 house designed by Richard Castle for Sir Marcus Beresford, Viscount and later Earl of Tyrone. It was an important house of the period and some of the interior plasterwork is by the skilled Francini brothers. The house was bought by the Government in 1835 and, partly altered, now houses a section of the Department of Education. A nineteenth-century replica of the house, fifty metres to the north, was destroyed in a fire in 1998 but has since been rebuilt. The area north-east of here was once known as 'Monto', a red-light district which features in James Joyce's *Ulysses*.

Return to the central mall on O'Connell Street. Across the street are the premises of Dublin Bus, where you can purchase a wide range of excursion and commuter tickets. The next monument is that of **Father Theobald Mathew**, apostle of temperance. In 1838, he signed a pledge of total abstinence and began an abstinence campaign around Ireland. He enjoyed remarkable success – half the adult population were disciples at one stage. Revenue on duties on spirits fell from £1.4 million to £0.8 million and there was a parallel reduction in crime.

On your right is the **Savoy Cinema**, which first opened in 1929. It is now the only cinema on a street which once boasted seven cinemas. Walk for fifty metres and look over at the **Gresham Hotel**, which opened in 1817. The original building was destroyed in the 1922 Civil War and the present one was constructed in the late 1920s. Perhaps the very place for a mid-tour refreshment stop.

Across the street, beside the Royal Dublin Hotel, is number **42**

**O'Connell Street**, the only surviving Georgian townhouse on the entire street. The red-brick building was designed by Richard Castle in 1752 and offers a tantalising glimpse of what the houses along Gardiner's Mall looked like. The house now belongs to the adjoining hotel.

Continue to a point directly opposite the main door of the Royal Dublin Hotel and cross to the right to **Cathal Brugha Street**, named after a Second-in-command during the 1916 Easter Rising. Brugha took a leading part in the War of Independence and was Chief of Staff of the IRA 1917-19. He voted against the Treaty of 1922 and, in the resulting Civil War, was involved in a shoot-out with Free State troops, during which he and his men occupied the nearby Gresham Hotel. In the skirmish, he was shot and later died from his wounds, on 7 July 1922.

The interesting building seventy

Lamppost
detail

metres down Cathal Brugha Street on the left is the parish church of **St George and St Thomas**. The 1931 Lombardo-Romanesque design was awarded the first Royal Institute of Architects of Ireland (RIAI) Gold Medal in 1935. Latter day, characterless and out-of-scale development in the vicinity has taken away its physical context and as a result the church seems a little lost here. In front of the church is a memorial to those who lost their lives in the Dublin Bombings on 17 May 1974. Thirty-four civilians were killed in two massive explosions in the north inner city in what was – until the 1998 Omagh tragedy – the worst atrocity of the Northern 'Troubles', north and south of the Border. Return to the central mall and walk to the end of the street. Directly ahead is the **Parnell Monument**.

Charles Stewart Parnell was born at Avondale in County Wicklow in 1846. He became a Home Rule MP for County Meath in 1875 and subsequently became president of the Home Rule Confederation of Great Britain, president of the Irish National Land League, and leader of the Irish Parliamentary Party in Westminster. He campaigned tirelessly for land reform in Ireland. After the election of 1885, Parnell and his eighty-five MPs held the balance of power at Westminster. His reputation earned him the title of 'The Chief' and 'The uncrowned king of Ireland'. In 1889, however, he was cited as a co-respondent in a divorce action brought by an Irish

# Around O'Connell Street

MP, Captain William O'Shea. O'Shea's wife, Katherine (Kitty), had been romantically involved with Parnell since 1880. The subsequent divorce scandal split the parliamentary party and Parnell was voted out of the leadership. He left Ireland with Kitty to live in Brighton, but died shortly after at the early age of forty-five.

Cross to the monument, a splendid work by Irish-born sculptor Augustus St Gaudens, in collaboration with the New York architect Henry Bacon, best known for the Lincoln Memorial in Washington. It was sculpted in New York, transported to Dublin and unveiled in front of over 100,000 people on the twentieth anniversary of Parnell's death in 1911. It is easily the finest monument on O'Connell Street. The three-sided obelisk is built of two Galway granites – Barna (the bollards and the curved slabs between the cobble-stones) and Shantalla (the obelisk itself). The bronze figure of Parnell is in typical oratorical pose. An interesting, unrelated fact is that some of the first Easter Rising prisoners laid down their arms at the Parnell Monument.

Cross to the **Ambassador Cinema**, originally the Rotunda Room and adjoining the nearby Rotunda Hospital. The entire area around **Parnell Square** is essential touring and you can turn to the *Northside Georgian* tour on page [**59**] if you wish to explore the buildings around the square.

For this tour, go left from the cinema and walk along **Parnell Street** and past the **Rotunda**

**Lying-In Hospital** on your right [**60**]. Across the street are two well-known Dublin pubs, the **Parnell Mooney** and **Conway's**. At the corner, cross to the left of Parnell Street and continue, taking the next left into **Moore Street**. Patrick Pearse surrendered to General Lowe at this point in 1916. Walk up Moore Street, a street traders' area and filled with the odour of fresh fish, fruit and vegetables. Pass on your right one of the entrances to the **ILAC Centre Shopping Mall**.

At the end of the street, look right along Henry Street. Two long-standing department stores – institutions, really – are facing each other – **Arnott's** and **Roches Stores**. Turn left and walk to the top of Henry Street and turn right at the GPO into O'Connell Street. Walk towards O'Connell Bridge.

At the junction with **Middle Abbey Street**, just beyond Eason's, divert briefly right and stop outside the side entrance to Eason's. At your feet is a pavement plaque, one of fourteen tracing the footsteps of Leopold Bloom in the eighth chapter of Joyce's *Ulysses*. This is the first of the plaques and you can follow them across O'Connell Bridge to the National Museum on Kildare Street.

Continue along O'Connell Street and cross the bridge. On the pavement, as you step onto the bridge, is another in the series of *Ulysses* pavement plaques. This one reads: '*As he set foot on O'Connell Bridge, a puffball of smoke plumed up from the parapet.*' Return to Bewley's to finish the tour.

**23**

Many of the old buildings which make up the narrow and intimate streetscapes in Temple Bar were built in the eighteenth century. Dublin's Custom House was then situated where now stands the Clarence Hotel on Wellington Quay and some buildings backed directly onto the river. In those days ships sailed up the Liffey, docking near Grattan Bridge. The district was a hive of activity, day and night.

Two hundred years later, as a result of massive investment and the implementation of a major development plan throughout the 1990s, Temple Bar is once more a thriving community. It has become a major tourist attraction and a significant addition to the city's cultural focus.

The best – and quietest – time to do this tour is Sunday morning.

## Tour Facts

- **Length:** 2 miles (3.2 kilometres)
- **Duration:** a leisurely 1½ hours
- **Refreshments:** during the tour (it's multi-choice time); after the tour (it's still multi-choice time)
- **Getting to the Starting Point:** from O'Connell Bridge, walk south along Westmoreland Street until you get to College Green; from Grafton Street, walk along the left of the lower end of the street, towards Trinity College, until you get to College Green

## Opening Times

- **Dublin's Viking Adventure**
  Telephone: (01) 679 6040
  Tues–Sat 10am–4.30pm (tours every half-hour)
  Closed Sunday and Monday
- **Temple Bar Information Centre**
  Telephone (01) 671 5717
  <u>June–August</u>
  Mon–Fri 9am–6pm
  Saturday 11am–4pm
  Sunday 12pm–4pm
  <u>September–May</u>
  Mon–Fri 9am–6pm
- **House of Lords**
  Telephone: (01) 677 6801
  Mon–Fri 10am–4pm (Thursday till 5pm)
  Closed all other times

**Tour begins:** *at the Henry Grattan monument on College Green pedestrian island, directly opposite the front gates of Trinity College.*

A dramatic location at which to begin the tour. John Henry Foley's fine statue of Grattan, *the* influential parliamentarian in the years preceding the Act of Union in 1800, faces Trinity College. To his right, College Green sweeps south towards Grafton Street.

Behind him stretches College Green and Dame Street to 'the old city'. To his left, the magnificent Bank of Ireland, formerly the House of Parliament [53]. Take a look at the two fine street lamps on either side of Grattan, with the three sea urchins and the

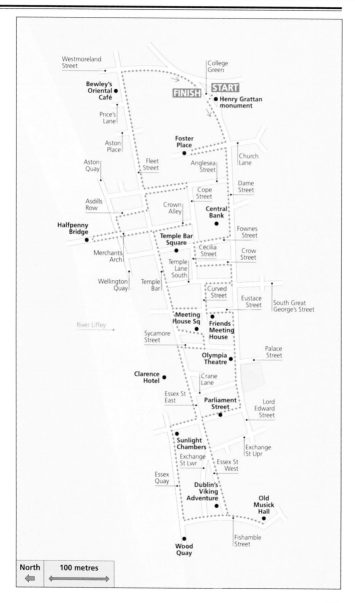

Westmoreland Street

College Green

Bewley's Oriental Café

**FINISH** **START**

● Henry Grattan monument

Price's Lane

Aston Place

Foster Place
●

Church Lane

Aston Quay

Fleet Street

Anglesea Street

Dame Street

Asdills Row

Cope Street

Crown Alley

Central Bank
●

Halfpenny Bridge

Fownes Street

Temple Bar Square

Cecilia Street

Crow Street

Merchants Arch

Temple Lane South

Wellington Quay

Temple Bar

Curved Street

Eustace Street

South Great George's Street

River Liffey

Meeting House Sq

Friends Meeting House

Sycamore Street

Olympia Theatre

Palace Street

Clarence Hotel
●

Crane Lane

Essex St East

Parliament Street

Lord Edward Street

Sunlight Chambers

Exchange St Lwr

Exchange St Upr

Essex St West

Essex Quay

Dublin's Viking Adventure

Old Musick Hall

Wood Quay

Fishamble Street

North

100 metres

characteristic three castles on the base representing Dublin Corporation, the city authority.

Cross the street to the Bank of Ireland side and turn left and walk past the front portico of the bank. Across to your left, in the centre of the street, is a 1966 sculpture by Edward Delaney commemorating the patriot **Thomas Davis** [103] and his Young Irelanders who attempted to reverse the Act of Union of 1800.

Turn right into **Foster Place**, a short, cobble-stoned, secluded cul-de-sac, named in 1792 after John Foster, Baron Oriel, the last Speaker of the Irish House of Commons between 1785 and 1800. Foster was a strong opponent of Catholic Emancipation and the Act of Union. The building facing you, with the carved cannon guns on top, was formerly the armoury of the Bank and is now the home of the Bank of Ireland Arts Centre. During the year, this is a venue for lunchtime music recitals. On your right is the western section of the old Parliament, built in 1797 and usually attributed to Robert Parke, with initial design work by James Gandon. On the left is number 3/4 Foster Place, formerly the home of the Hibernian United Services Club, later the headquarters of the Royal Bank of Ireland, and now a banking branch of Allied Irish Bank.

Rejoin College Green. Directly across the street is the short and narrow Church Lane, at the top of which you can see St Andrew's Church, recently converted to house the city's main tourist information centre. Continue to number 3 College Green, present home of stockbrokers and an accountancy firm and the site of an infamous and long-defunct Dublin gambling house, Daly's Club. It was particularly notorious during the late 1700s, when it was connected to the old Parliament by an underground passageway.

Continue to **Anglesea Street**, on the right, named after Arthur Annesley, first Earl of Anglesea, who bought the land on which Anglesea Street sits from Dublin Corporation in the seventeenth century. Thirty metres down on the left is Blooms Hotel, named after Leopold Bloom, the principal character in James Joyce's *Ulysses*. Closing off the view at the end of the street is a distant snapshot of the northern Liffey quays.

Continue along College Green, which becomes Dame Street by the time you reach the Central Bank Plaza. Sit on any of the seats near the Golden Tree ('Crann an Óir') sculpture. Look right, at the **Commercial Buildings** (the name is above the entrance), originally built in 1796 and, until their re-alignment, facing south onto Dame Street. They were the headquarters of the Dublin Chamber of Commerce between 1799 and 1964. When the Central Bank was being built, the Commercial Buildings were dismantled, brick by brick, each brick being numbered. The intention was to re-assemble the building in its present position and aspect; however a completely new 'original' was built in its place.

The **Central Bank** was built

between 1972 and 1978 and was designed by Dublin's most controversial modern architect, Sam Stephenson. Its enormous bulk dwarfs its nearest neighbours and is aggressive in a locality which has always been small in scale. If Stephenson was looking for notice, he succeeded here, but he didn't win many friends. All that being said, the building does have considerable architectural merits – it's just a pity that both the bank and its architect were intent on making such an inappropriately large statement, instead of attempting to blend in with the surroundings. As for the plaza, watch out for the wind tunnels on blustery days. I'm sure you did not come to Dublin to learn to fly, but you may have no choice in the matter. The bank caused quite a stir during its construction due to its suspended structure – it was built from the top down.

Now, walk along Dame Street and turn right at the end of the plaza into **Fownes Street**. On the corner is a splendid 1868 building in a Lombardo-Romanesque style, by the noted architect Thomas Newenham Deane. It has very recently been plucked from obscurity and years of neglect and is now the modern Trinity Arch Hotel. An uninterrupted terrace of some of the oldest buildings in Temple Bar line Fownes Street along here. Some of them are important examples of an early eighteenth-century panelled house type which is now very rare in Dublin.

At the end of the terrace, turn left into **Cecilia Street**, named

Meeting House Square

after St Cecilia, the patron saint of music. The newspaper, The Dublin Penny Journal, had its offices here in 1835. Mid-way down Cecilia Street on the right is **Cecilia House [67]**, which stands on the site of an Augustinian Friary, founded in 1259 and later, the Crow Street Theatre (1757-1820). There are plans to change the building's present use to that of a forty-one-bedroomed hotel, with a bar which will be devoted to activities related to Irish culture and the Irish language. Two doors down from Cecilia House is Claddagh Records, a specialist outlet for traditional music. Between these two buildings is a former warehouse, typical of many small warehouse buildings in Temple Bar in the seventeenth and eighteenth century.

Go left up **Crow Street**, opposite Cecilia House. The street is typical Temple Bar, with its mix of old warehouses, timber-framed shopfronts and new infill buildings. Like Fownes Street and Temple Lane (which you will visit shortly), Crow Street was traditionally associated with the clothing trade – drapers, merchant tailors, woollen merchants, cap makers, furriers and military tailors. Mid-way up on the right is the **Green Building**, designed to accommodate a variety of environmental principles, including wind and solar energy. It incorporates a wide range of recycled materials in its structure and is among the city's most interesting modern buildings. It is easily identifiable by the pale green copper door, with insc portholes, and an old toilet cistern connected to over twenty old tap. and water pipes.

Turn right at the top and walk past Temple Lane South and stop opposite **South Great George's Street** to the left. The splendid corner building diagonally right, faced with terracotta tiles, was formerly a Burton's clothing shop and is currently home to the charity, Rehab, though the building has a 'For Sale' sign as I write. Two hundred metres up South Great George's Street on the left is a large, red-brick Victorian building, designed in 1881 as the **South City Markets**. It was rebuilt in 1892 after a fire which destroyed much of the original. It is a much overlooked building, which is surprising as it is one of the city's most beautiful.

Retrace your steps a few metres and turn left into **Temple Lane South**, once named Dirty Lane and before that, Hogges Lane. Donegan's, a famous Irish watch manufacturer, left this street in 1982 having produced over 20,000 watches in its workshop since production began in 1820. The back of the Green Building is on

the right (more recycled designs), as is the Square Wheel Cycleworks, a workers' co-operative project run by cyclists for cyclists. It offers a supervised cycle-park facility.

Go left into the newly-constructed, limestone-surfaced **Curved Street**, which houses Arthouse, a multimedia centre for the arts, and the Temple Bar Music Centre.

Directly ahead is a passageway which leads down shallow steps into Meeting House Square which you will visit later. Go left up **Eustace Street**, named after Sir Maurice Eustace, speaker of the House of Commons in 1639. His house and gardens once occupied the site on which this street was laid out. On the right, number 6 is the Irish Film Centre (IFC) and next to this is the Quaker **Friends Meeting House**. A wall plaque states that the *'Society of United Irishmen of Dublin was founded on 9th November 1791 at the Eagle Tavern on this site'*. Parts of the IFC building date from the Quakers' arrival in Ireland in 1692.

Turn right at the top. There is a cluster of ethnic restaurants on both sides of Dame Street along here. Cross **Sycamore Street** – where Joshua Bewley started his tea importation business around 1840 – to the **Olympia Theatre**. This opened in 1879 as the Star of Erin Music Hall and became known as Dan Lowry's after its founder. The Victorian canopy in glass and ironwork is an appropriate entrance to a slightly shabby but otherwise charming Victorian theatre interior. Directly across Dame Street is an Allied Irish Bank. The Italian baroque style building was designed by Sir Thomas Newenham Deane in 1872 and extended in the 1950s using a different limestone, from Ardbraccan in County Meath. The original building used Ballinasloe limestone, from County Galway. Can you see where the old building joins the new one? At the side of the AIB is Palace Street which leads into the Lower Castle Yard of Dublin Castle [**67**].

Beside Palace Street is a small public garden overlooked by three statues. These are said to represent crafts in wood, metal and stone and were formerly part of the façade of the long-since defunct Exhibition Palace in Earlsfort Terrace, where now stands the National Concert Hall. In this vicinity a dam once controlled the tide flow where the River Poddle joined the Black Pool [**68**] at the back of Dublin Castle. Later, the medieval church of St Mary del Dam was founded here. Dame Street's name is derived from both the original dam and the later church.

Continue for a hundred metres to the traffic lights. Straight ahead is Lord Edward Street, with Christ Church Cathedral [**71**] in the distance. Immediately to your left is City Hall, formerly the Royal Exchange [**42**]. Just up the hill is the newly restored Newcomen's Bank, now offices of Dublin Corporation.

Turn right into the attractive **Parliament Street [42]**, established in 1757 by an Act of Parliament which granted £12,000 'for the acquisition and

construction of the new street'. In past times, it was known for its cabinet-making traditions and was also home to many eighteenth-century printers and publishers. As recently as the early 1990s, it was very run-down: however, careful restoration and sensitive development have protected it from the ravages other city streets have suffered over the past thirty years. The attractive Thomas Read's Bar and Café [**150**] is on the corner, beside what was, until its closure in 1997, Dublin's oldest shop, established as a cutlers in 1670 and named 'Read's Surgical Instrument Maker and Cutler to Her Majesty'. There are plans by the current owners to restore the entire building and re-open 'Dublin's oldest shop'.

Across the street, at number 33/34, The Front Lounge [**150**] is housed in a particularly attractive building. The lounge itself is unusual in its layout and décor and is well worth a visit.

There is an interesting variety of small shops and galleries on the street. You can even find out what you will be doing tomorrow in the House of Astrology. Hopefully, you will not be requiring the services of Victim Support which provides, among other services, support to victims of tourist crime. The strangely named Turk's Head Chop House [**150**] on the left was not established in 1760, as the sign above one of the windows indicates. Maybe the original licence was handed out in 1760, but I can assure you that *this* pub is not 240 years old!

Cross to the left side of Parliament Street at the pedestrian

Gigging in Temple Bar

architectural design – by that man, Sam Stephenson, again! – but also because they were built on top of highly significant archaeological remains from early Viking Dublin [**74**].

At the end of Essex Street West, running at right angles, is **Fishamble Street**, birthplace of Henry Grattan and of the poet James Clarence Mangan [**98**]. On the right-hand corner of Fishamble and Essex is a late seventeenth-century house, believed to be Dublin's oldest inhabited house. Go left, up to the George Frideric Handel Hotel, beside which, to your left, is a plaque which explains that Handel's Oratorio *Messiah* was first performed in the **Old Musick Hall** (demolished) at noon on Tuesday 13 April 1742. Handel himself conducted that first performance to a packed house. In pre-concert publicity ladies were advised not to wear hoops and men were asked not to bring their swords, evidence that a large crowd was expected. Admission was half a guinea and, according to the post-concert notices, the musical event was a huge success. Look up the hill at the north side of Christ Church Cathedral before retracing your footsteps, down to the end of Fishamble Street and onto Wood Quay.

lights and walk up **Essex Gate**, along the side of the Turk's Head. Exchange Street Lower, which winds around to the right, was formerly known as Blind Quay. Proceed in a straight line towards **Essex Street West**. To your immediate left is **Exchange Street Upper**, at the top of which is a nice view of Newcomen's Bank and, beyond, the old gate into Dublin Castle with the State Apartments in the background.

Continue along Essex Street West. To your right is **Dublin's Viking Adventure**, occupying the old St Michael and St John Church. Smock Alley Court on the right is a modern apartment building and is named after the **Smock Alley Theatre** which was built here in 1661 and closed in the 1790s. Extensive and quite recent archaeological excavations uncovered much of the theatre's fabric. Directly ahead are the dual buildings of the **Civic Offices** of Dublin Corporation (from where you are standing, you can see only one), commonly referred to as the 'Bunkers'. They are controversial, not only for their unusual

**Wood Quay** is the oldest river quay in Dublin and was named after the large wooden supports behind which land was reclaimed for the establishment of a quayside, around the year 1200. Take stock here, look around, get your bearings. The second phase buildings of the Civic Offices are on your left, emblazoned with the words Bárdas Átha Cliath (Dublin Corporation). Across the river to your left is the Four Courts, with its large copper-green dome. Beyond it is the smaller dome of St Paul's Church. Across the river to your right run the Liffey Quays downriver towards O'Connell Bridge and Dublin Bay.

Turn right and walk past the half-buried Viking ship beside the bus stop, entitled *'Baite'* and sculpted by Betty Maguire. Behind this is the façade of the now transformed Franciscan church of **St Michael and St John**. Built in 1815, it had a fine Gothic interior and was Dublin's oldest Roman Catholic church until its last mass was said in April 1990.

Continue to the corner of Parliament Street. Stand at the edge of the footpath on Parliament Street and look up at the terracotta carvings on the side of the Lombardo-Romanesque **Sunlight Chambers** building. Built around 1900 by Lever Brothers, the soap manufacturers, the carvings describe the history of soap and hygiene. The bridge spanning the Liffey at this point is Grattan Bridge [**42**] and is modelled on Westminster Bridge in London. Across the street is The Porter House [**150**], an interesting pub which brews, on the premises, its own beers.

Cross Parliament Street and walk down **Essex Street East** into the heart of Temple Bar. The name 'Temple Bar' derives from the Temple family, whose figurehead, Sir William Temple, had been Provost of Trinity College in 1609. The family owned a house and gardens between present-day Anglesea and Eustace Streets, in the early seventeenth century.

**Dolphin House**, twenty metres down on the right, was once the Dolphin Hotel and Restaurant, a thriving establishment and especially popular among the legal profession. It was designed by J.J. O'Callaghan in 1898. It has since been converted into offices. On your left is the back entrance to the popular **Clarence Hotel**, owned by the rock group, U2. The hotel occupies the approximate site of the original Custom House (1707-91), before Gandon built his masterpiece on Custom House Quay. Directly opposite is **Crampton Court**, a rarely used and uninviting old laneway which leads to Dame Street. It is named after a well-known clock-making family, who developed the area around here between 1700 and 1751. Beside Crampton Court is Connolly Books, a left-wing bookshop with a regular clientele and many passersby dropping in to browse.

Go right up Sycamore Street and left after twenty metres into **Meeting House Square**, a new structural addition to Temple Bar and named after the former Quaker Meeting House where now sits the Irish Film Centre, and also after a former Presbyterian Meeting House in the building now occupied by The Ark on Eustace Street. A lively, open-air market takes place in the square every Saturday. During the summer months, a large screen reveals itself above the Gallery of Photography and open-air cinema comes to Dublin. Immediately to your right, steps lead to the Irish Film Centre. Directly across the square from where you entered are shallow steps which lead to Eustace Street and beyond to the Curved Street. To the left of the steps is the rear of The Ark, the front of which you will see shortly. The shutters on the building open to reveal a stage for concerts, children's theatre and other entertainment events.

Exit the square to the left, back onto Essex Street. Directly opposite is **Designyard**, one of Temple Bar's many cultural flagships, where contemporary jewellery, furniture, ceramics, glass and textiles is on exhibit and for sale in a converted, previously derelict Victorian warehouse. The four iron gates on the front of the building were designed by Irish sculptor Kathy Prendergast and fabricated by Harry Page. The gates are based on maps of four cities: Dublin, Madrid, New York and Vienna. Inside, the colourful mosaic meandering the length of the ground floor is an artistic reflection of the River Poddle, which flows underneath.

Continue along Essex Street, passing on your left Fitzsimons Bar, a popular venue for live traditional music and dancing. Diagonally opposite, on the corner, is The Norseman, an old Dublin pub which fell foul of the modernisation trend in Temple Bar and has lost its architectural integrity, if not custom. Outside the pub, on Eustace Street, is Winifred's Well, recently uncovered and restored but going largely unnoticed by the Temple

Bar throng. Several buildings up Eustace Street, in number 18, is the **Temple Bar Information Centre** in what was formerly a derelict eighteenth-century townhouse, believed to have been a 'Counting House' or private bank. Inside, you can pick up a lot more information on Temple Bar than I have the space for here. Next door, number 17 is a restored eighteenth-century townhouse with timber-panelled interiors. Across the street is **The Ark**, an arts resource for children in a converted printing works and warehouse. The original building had been a Presbyterian Meeting House and all but the 1725 façade had been rebuilt long before the Temple Bar renewal scheme got under way.

Go back to the Norseman and turn right. You are entering the most commercial part of Temple Bar. The **Black Church Print Studio** (closed Sundays and Mondays) is on your left, an original print gallery occupying a new, four-storey building. Beside this is the **Temple Bar Gallery and Studios** (closed Mondays), founded in 1983. It is the largest studio and gallery complex in the country, with working space for thirty full-time, professional artists working in sculpture, painting, printing, photography and multi-media. Diagonally opposite is **Temple Bar Square**. This public space, occupying what had been a derelict site and surface car park for many years, is arguably the least successful of all that has happened in Temple Bar since its latter day renewal. It is a cold, uninviting space and can be rowdy and unpleasant at night time.

Cross the square and go up **Crown Alley**. On the left, half-way up, is a beautifully restored nineteenth-century warehouse, featuring skilfully executed cut stonework, stone archways and decorative brickwork. Along the top is a signboard running the length of the building, telling you that the warehouse was once owned by A. Oman & Sons. You will find that your eyes are reluctantly drawn upwards to the domineering Central Bank, aggressively bearing down on what should be an intimate streetscape.

Go back down Crown Alley and through the lively **Merchants Arch** (1821) to the **Halfpenny (Ha'penny) Bridge** spanning the Liffey. The footbridge, originally named Wellington Bridge and later changed to Liffey Bridge, was built in 1816: users were charged a toll of one halfpenny (ha'penny) until 1919. Standing in the middle, over the Liffey, you can see, looking east and downriver, O'Connell Bridge, Liberty Hall, the Custom House and the Financial Services Centre. Looking west and upstream, you can see, on the south (left) side of the river, the dome of Adam and Eve Church and, in the centre of your line of vision, the copper-green dome of the Onion Tower in the Guinness Brewery. On the north side, you can see the dome of the Four Courts.

Go back to the entrance to Merchants Arch, turn left down the quays and immediately right into Asdills Row. An interesting residential scheme, **Crampton Buildings** (1890), is neatly tucked away to the left. At the end of Asdill's Row, turn left into **Fleet Street**. Continue past numerous restaurants and pubs and turn right at The Auld Dubliner into **Anglesea Street**. There are many fine late nineteenth/early twentieth-century houses along here, number 10 on the right being particularly attractive, with its rectangular bay window on the first floor and fine decorations on the building's façade. The **Irish Stock Exchange**, across the street, has traded here since 1878, its original home having been the Royal Exchange, now City Hall.

Return to Fleet Street and turn right. Thirty metres down on the left is a wall plaque stating that the patriot Kevin Barry was born 'in this house' on 20 January 1902. He was hanged in 1920, following his capture during an IRA raid on a military lorry in Church Street. The building here looks somewhat more recent than 1902 and perhaps the plaque should read 'in a house on this site'.

Continue to the corner of Price's Lane and stop and admire the ornate side façade of **Bewley's Oriental Café [11]**. Beside Bewley's is one of Dublin's more interesting pubs, the **Palace Bar [142]**. Turn right into Westmoreland Street and go past the **House of Lords** entrance to the Bank of Ireland, with its splendid Corinthian columns. To finish the tour, continue walking around the bank until you reach College Green, the starting point for this tour.

Dublin is blessed with a variety of parks, large and small. Many are mentioned throughout this book. The three parks on this tour are in the south inner city and each one offers something quite individual to the visitor.

St Stephen's Green is Dublin's most popular park. On warm, sunny days it is filled with people – strolling, sitting, stretched out on the grass. A visit to Iveagh Gardens is like stepping into a parallel world, where the noise of the city is barely audible and the sight of more than a dozen or so visitors is rare. Merrion Square is in the heart of Georgian Dublin. It is surrounded by, on three sides, splendid Georgian townhouses and, on the fourth, by fine public buildings.

## Tour Facts

- **Length of tour:** 2 miles (3.2 kilometres)
- **Duration of tour:** 1 hour, with no rests
- **Refreshments:** during the tour (Shelbourne Hotel; O'Donoghue's pub); after the tour (Mont Clare Hotel; Davenport Hotel; Doheny & Nesbitt's pub; Toner's pub)
- **Getting to the Starting Point:** walk to the top (south) of Grafton Street

## Opening Times

- **St Stephen's Green**
  Telephone (01) 661 3111
  Weekdays 8am; Sunday/Public Holidays 10am
  Closes 20 minutes before darkness
- **Iveagh Gardens**
  Telephone (01) 661 3111
  Open 10am all year round
  Closes 6pm in summer; before dark during rest of year
- **Merrion Square**
  Telephone (01) 661 2369
  Open daily 8am till dusk

**Tour begins:** *at the Fusiliers' Arch (the main entrance to St Stephen's Green, across from the top of Grafton Street).*

### St Stephen's Green

Dublin's most popular public park, St Stephen's Green (henceforth referred to in this tour as the Green) is a pure delight. It was formally laid out and opened to the public in 1880 by Arthur Edward Guinness, then proprietor of the Guinness Brewery and later to become Lord Ardilaun. Prior to that the Green had been enclosed since 1663 when for a time the west side was a place of execution and adjacent to a nearby leper colony. During the latter half of the eighteenth century, the aristocracy strolled in their elegant attire along the

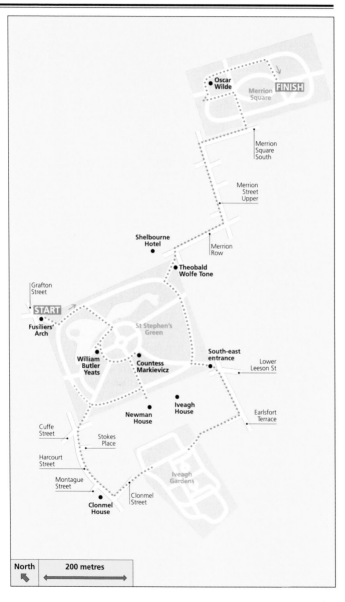

Oscar
Wilde

Merrion
Square

**FINISH**

Merrion
Square
South

Merrion
Street
Upper

Shelbourne
Hotel

Merrion
Row

Theobald
Wolfe Tone

Grafton
Street

**START**

Fusiliers'
Arch

St Stephen's
Green

South-east
entrance

Lower
Leeson St

William
Butler
Yeats

Countess
Markievicz

Iveagh
House

Earlsfort
Terrace

Newman
House

Cuffe
Street

Stokes
Place

Iveagh
Gardens

Harcourt
Street

Montague
Street

Clonmel
Street

Clonmel
House

North

200 metres

pavement outside the Green on warm summer evenings and dry Sunday afternoons. Each of the four sides had its own named 'walk', the most fashionable being the Beaux Walk, on the north side, along where the Shelbourne Hotel is today. The others were Leeson Walk (south), Monks Walk (east) and French Walk (west). For those interested in statistics, the Green's area is 8.8 hectares, or 22 acres.

Begin the first of two visits to the Green by passing underneath the **Fusiliers' Arch**. This memorial arch commemorates the 212 Irish soldiers of the Royal Dublin Fusiliers who died in the Boer War of 1899-1902.

Ahead of you is a section of the large ornamental pond which accounts for a significant portion of the northern area of the park. Mallard and moorhen are the most common waterfowl to be found here.

Walk to the water's edge and go left along the lake and turn right onto the bridge. This is the second O'Connell Bridge in Dublin and, as Michael Caine might say, 'not many people know that'. Descend to the central, circular gardens. The pleasing landscape design is usually ablaze with the startling colours of a wide variety of flowering plants, routinely dug up and replaced with different varieties and patterns by a team of hard-working gardeners. The scene is further enhanced by the unusual fountains, with their bronze lotus flowers and bulrush spouting water throughout the day.

Walk right, around the perimeter of this central section, to the pagoda-style rain shelter. Beside the shelter are stone steps which lead up to a clearing in the lush growth. At the far end of the clearing is a statue by Henry Moore of the poet **William Butler Yeats [110]**, erected in 1967. The sculpture is not signposted, so the area here offers the visitor an unusual haven of tranquillity. On a warm, sunny day it is a nice place to sit and rest awhile. Go back down the steps and continue along the curved path. After ten metres, stop and look at the bust of **James Clarence Mangan [98]**, a Dublin poet who lived and died in abject poverty. Just beyond the bust is a map detailing the location of all the monuments in the Green. Continue for thirty metres to another bust, that of **Countess Markievicz.**

Countess Markievicz was born Constance Gore-Booth in London in 1868 and educated by a governess at Lissadell in County Sligo. In 1900 she married a Polish count whom she had met while studying art in Paris. They settled in Dublin in 1903. In 1908 she became committed to the nationalist cause and joined Sinn Féin. During the 1916 Easter Rising, she served as a major at the nearby College of Surgeons under Michael Mallin. Subsequently condemned to death, her sentence was commuted and, in the general amnesty of 1917, she was released. In 1918 she became the first woman to be elected to the British House of Commons, however in keeping with Sinn

Tranquil scene in St Stephen's Green

Féin's policy she refused to take her seat. During the 'Troubles' – the common term which described the years of struggle before independence – she was constantly on the run and served two jail sentences. A fierce opponent of the Anglo-Irish Treaty of 1921, she joined the Fianna Fáil Party, founded by Eamon de Valera, in 1926. She was re-elected to the Irish Parliament in 1927 but, in failing health, died later that year.

From the Markievicz bust, go back fifteen metres, turn left and walk along the straight path, past the bandstand on your right. At the end of the path, on your right, is a bronze bust of **James Joyce** [**111**], by the sculptor Marjorie Fitzgibbon, in 1982. Briefly leave the Green by the narrow gate in front of you. The seat nearby on the pavement commemorates James and his father, John Stanislaus Joyce, and faces **Newman House** [**46**], where James attended college at the turn of the century. Adjacent to Newman House is the archway entrance to **University Church** (1855-6), a Byzantine basilica and popular church among post-graduates of University College Dublin (UCD) for marriage ceremonies. To the left of Newman House, fifty metres along the Green, is **Iveagh House** [**47**], once the home of Sir Benjamin Lee Guinness and now home to the Department of Foreign Affairs.

Return to the park by the same gate and walk left along the inner perimeter path until you reach Ardilaun Lodge, the head gardener's house occupying the south-western corner. From here, if you look right, you can see the seated figure of Lord Ardilaun looking across to the College of Surgeons (not in view).

*[Brief diversion: Walk over to Lord Ardilaun's statue and view the College of Surgeons [46]. Retrace your steps.]*

Leave the Green by the corner

House on Parnell Square [**59**]. Turn left into Clonmel Street and enter **Iveagh Gardens**, a relatively small park and easy to explore. Enjoy it in your own time and continue the tour when the mood takes you.

<u>IVEAGH GARDENS</u>
**Originally the private gardens of nearby Clonmel House, Iveagh Gardens were for a time in the nineteenth century pleasure gardens, before being redesigned and planted by Ninian Niven around the time the Dublin Exhibition took place here in 1863. At that time, they were called the Coburg Gardens. Not long after, they were acquired by Lord Iveagh, proprietor of the Guinness Brewery, and they remained in his possession until the early 1940s, when the house and gardens were acquired by the State. The State in turn handed the gardens to University College Dublin.**

*Iveagh Gardens* gate, admiring the gardens of Ardilaun Lodge as you pass. Cross at the pedestrian lights directly ahead and go up **Harcourt Street**, on the left. On the far side, number 4 is the birthplace of Edward Henry Carson (1854-1935), regarded as the founder of modern Unionism. He is also remembered as the barrister who cross-examined Oscar Wilde in Wilde's unsuccessful legal action against the Marquis of Queensbury. The house, or rather the shell, has recently been retrieved from what had seemed, for many years, inevitable demolition. On the same side, at number 14, the eighteenth-century chronicler Sir Jonah Barrington (1760-1834) lived. A few doors up, at number 17, Clonmel House was home to the Municipal Gallery of Modern Art, founded by Sir Hugh Lane, from 1908 to 1932. The museum is now housed in Charlemont

Truly, you have entered a tranquil oasis in the heart of the city. High walls surrounding the Gardens are the cornerstone of this tranquillity; the tall buildings on three of its sides further consolidate this feeling. Quiet and understated, the beauty is everywhere, particularly in the many fine trees, mainly horse chestnut, ash, pine and plane, as well as the prolific holly trees, some of which have grown to unusually large sizes around the south-eastern corner.

When you enter the Gardens, you'll see a straight path running across the park directly ahead. This leads to the only other entrance and exit to the Gardens and is the one which you will be using when you have decided to move on.

To your left is the 'archery ground'. This hollow has been the location of some of the most magical theatre seen in Dublin in recent times, with the travelling theatre group *Footsbarn* presenting imaginative interpretations of Homer's *Odyssey* and Shakespeare's *A Midsummer Night's Dream* inside a giant marquee. To the right is the central parterre with two simple but pleasing classical fountains and, further right, paths which lead to a rose garden and a curious maze, by the look of it, designed exclusively for leprechauns, though I have never seen one on my many visits.

When you leave the Gardens through the narrow gate at the eastern side, the rear of the National Concert Hall [**102**] confronts you. This was originally the main campus building of University College Dublin before the institution moved to a vast green space in the southern suburbs in the 1960s. Walk to the front of the building, turn left into Earlsfort Terrace and, when you reach the traffic lights, cross to the pedestrian island. To your right is Leeson Street which leads to the Victorian suburb of Donnybrook. Straight ahead is St Stephen's Green East, with a mixture of original Georgian and neo-Georgian buildings in a line. To your left is St Stephen's Green South, which you saw earlier.

Cross and enter the Green for the second time. Look at the map on your immediate right to help you get your bearings. Directly ahead is an interesting bronze sculpture of three female figures over a fountain, presented to the Irish Government in 1956 by West Germany in recognition of Irish aid after World War II. The figures represent the three fates, spinning and measuring the thread of man's destiny. Go right here and walk along the inner perimeter path to the next (north-eastern) corner. Along the way, have a look at the many fine trees. There are currently over 200 species of trees in the Green. Many of these are exotic varieties and there are plans to introduce more. Along this side are fine examples of native ash, holm oak, holly, Turkey oak, as well as London plane.

The two sculptures at the north-eastern corner are, inside the park, '**Famine**', a memorial by Edward Delaney to those who died from starvation in the 1845-8 Famine and, outside, the same sculptor's bronze statue of **Theobald Wolfe Tone**, leader of the United Irishmen and the insurrection of 1798, and of the failed French expedition to Ireland that same year.

Leave the Green here and look over at the **Shelbourne Hotel** [**105**], an elegant Victorian building overlooking the Green. The Constitution of the Irish Free State was drafted in the hotel in the early 1920s. Cross to the Shelbourne side of the street and go right, stopping briefly to look at the small, intimate cemetery on the left. It was founded by French Huguenot non-conformist churches of Dublin in 1693 and was restored during Dublin's Millennium year in 1988.

Continue, passing on your right O'Donoghue's pub [**151**] before turning left at the traffic lights into Merrion Street Upper. Number 24, across the street and anonymous now as a result of its integration with the new Merrion Hotel, is the birthplace of Arthur Wellesley, later to become the Duke of Wellington. Directly opposite what was number 24 is the main entrance to Government Buildings [**50**]. Continue. At the entrance to the Natural History Museum, cross to Merrion Square South and walk by the superb Georgian doorways, passing on your way former homes of George Russell (AE), William Butler Yeats [**110**] and Andrew O'Connor. Stop at number 76, cross the street and enter the park.

### MERRION SQUARE

**Archbishop Ryan Park, known to all Dubliners as Merrion Square [50], is today among the city's most beautiful parks, however for a long time it was very unclear what was going to happen to this tranquil green space in the centre of Georgian Dublin. The Archdiocese of Dublin finally abandoned its disastrous plans to construct a cathedral in the grounds when it leased the park to Dublin Corporation in 1974. Since then, the Parks Department of the Corporation have succeeded in creating a wonderful amenity for the people of Dublin – and its visitors.**

When you enter the park through this gate, you leave one world behind and enter another. The natural light of the day is severely hindered by the lush flora the moment you step off the pavement. Walk straight along the path ahead of you, passing busts to Michael Collins (left) and Henry Grattan (right), before turning left at the point where the park opens up into an oval shape on your right. Walk along this winding and ever-darkening corridor until you arrive at the back of the Rutland Fountain, designed in 1791 to commemorate the Duke of Rutland, a former Viceroy, and his wife. It has been recently restored. Ascend the few steps and cross to the railings and look across the street at the façade of the National Gallery [**51**] and to its left, the lawns of Leinster House [**48**].

Descend the steps you came up and turn left and follow this path until you arrive at one of the few imaginative, flamboyant and courageous modern sculptures in Dublin. Fitting, really, as **Oscar Wilde** was all of these and many more. The sculptor is Danny Osborne and he used forty different kinds of stone from many parts of the globe in this unusual creation. Oscar himself is lying on a massive slab of quartz

Merrion
Square

and is looking towards the family home at number I Merrion Square. It's the corner house, where Oscar lived from 1855 to 1878, from age one to twenty-four. Two sculpted figures, of his pregnant wife Constance and the Greek god of wine, Dionysius, sit on plinths on which are carved dozens of Wilde epigrams, each one in the handwriting of well-known Irish personalities. Before you leave, you might like to study Oscar's expression, first his left profile, next face-to-face and, finally, his right profile. (Dubliners, by the way, have nicknamed the sculpture *The Fag on the Crag [21]*).

For the remainder of your stay in the park your time, as in Iveagh Gardens, is your own. Explore the pathways and the open spaces and take time to sit for awhile on one of the many benches, soaking up the park's atmosphere. Look out for some of the twenty lampposts which once lit Dublin streets and are now lining the paths, thanks to the imagination of a Dublin Corporation official. The trees are a mixed bunch, many of them plane trees which were planted near the railings. The shrubs which line the railings and provide the shelter from the busy world outside are mainly holly and laurel.

To finish the tour, you might like to drop in to the nearby Mont Clare Hotel or the Davenport Hotel (opposite and beside the Wilde home, respectively) or, for something stronger, go back the way you came, turn left at the junction beyond the Merrion Hotel and visit either Doheny & Nesbitt's or Toner's [**151**], both traditional old Victorian pubs with exquisite interiors.

An interesting and enjoyable stroll around the heart of Georgian Dublin. Admire the fine period residences, now principally maintained for commercial use, the magnificent eighteenth-century public buildings and the graceful Georgian squares. Along the way, discover where many leading political and literary figures lived.

You can complete the tour in a morning or an afternoon, or you can make a day of it, visiting the State Apartments and Newman House in the morning, followed by lunch anywhere around the Grafton Street/Dawson Street area. In the afternoon, visit Number 29 Lower Fitzwilliam Street and the Old Library and Book of Kells in Trinity and, if the Bank of Ireland is still open by the time you reach it, drop in to see the House of Lords.

## Tour Facts

- **Length of tour:** 4.8 miles (7.7 kilometres)
- **Duration of tour:** a leisurely 2½ hours
- **Refreshments:** during the tour (the café in the National Museum); after the tour (Temple Bar is your oyster)
- **Getting to the Starting Point:** Grattan Bridge spans the Liffey between Capel Street and Parliament Street, one bridge west (upriver) of O'Connell Bridge (disregarding the Ha'penny Bridge)

**Tour begins:** *on the east (Dublin Bay) side of Grattan Bridge.*

From where you are standing, you can see the copper-green domes of two of the finest Georgian buildings in Ireland, the Four Courts and the Custom House, west and east respectively on the north Liffey Quays. Grattan Bridge was, in a previous incarnation, Essex Bridge, built in 1676 and rebuilt in 1753. The present bridge was built in 1875. Most Dubliners refer to it as Capel Street Bridge.

Cross onto Parliament Street and look across to Sunlight Chambers [**31**], on the opposite corner. It is easily identifiable by the terracotta friezes on first – and second-floor level. **Parliament Street [29]** is one of Dublin's most attractive thoroughfares. It was the first street to be laid out by the Wide Streets Commissioners (in 1762) and its construction opened up a route from Essex Bridge to Dublin Castle. Walk to the end of the street and look over at City Hall, which faces down Parliament Street.

Designed by Thomas Cooley as the Royal Exchange and built between 1769 and 1779 at a cost of £40,000, it was purchased by Dublin Corporation in 1851 and the following year renamed City

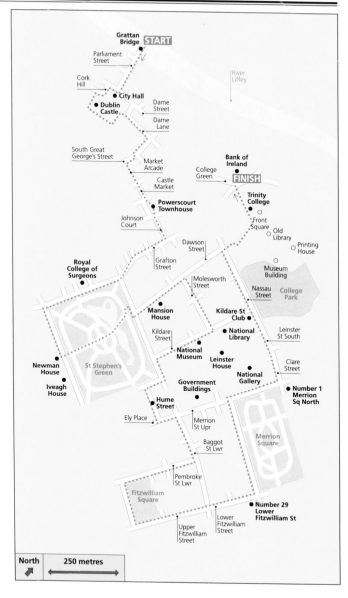

**Grattan Bridge** START

Parliament Street

Cork Hill

● City Hall

● Dublin Castle

Dame Street

Dame Lane

River Liffey

South Great George's Street

Market Arcade

Castle Market

**Bank of Ireland**

College Green

FINISH

**Trinity College**

**Powerscourt Townhouse**

○ Front Square

○ Old Library

○ Printing House

Johnson Court

Dawson Street

Grafton Street

Molesworth Street

○ Museum Building

**Royal College of Surgeons**

Nassau Street

College Park

**Mansion House**

**Kildare St Club** ●

Kildare Street

● **National Library**

Leinster St South

**National Museum**

**Leinster House**

Clare Street

**Newman House** ●

St Stephen's Green

**National Gallery**

● **Number 1 Merrion Sq North**

**Iveagh House** ●

**Government Buildings**

● **Hume Street**

Ely Place

Merrion St Upr

Merrion Square

Baggot St Lwr

Pembroke St Lwr

Fitzwilliam Square

Lower Fitzwilliam Street

● **Number 29 Lower Fitzwilliam St**

Upper Fitzwilliam Street

North

250 metres

## Opening Times

- **State Apartments**
  Telephone (01) 677 7129
  Mon–Fri 10am–5pm
  Sat/Sun/Bank Holidays:
  2pm–5pm

- **Powerscourt Townhouse Centre**
  Telephone (01) 679 4144
  Mon–Sat 9am–6pm (7pm on Thursday)
  Closed Sunday

- **Newman House**
  Telephone (01) 706 7422
  June–August
  Tues–Fri. 12pm–5pm
  Saturday 2pm–5pm
  Sunday 11am–2pm
  Closed Monday
  Phone to arrange visiting time during rest of the year

- **National Library**
  Telephone: (01) 661 8811
  Mon–Wed 10am–9pm
  Thurs–Fri 10am–4.45pm
  Saturday 10am–12.45pm
  Closed Sunday

- **National Museum**
  Telephone: (01) 677 7444
  Tues–Sat 10am–5pm
  Sunday 2pm–5pm
  Closed Monday

- **Number 29 Lower Fitzwilliam Street**
  Telephone: (01) 702 6165
  Tues–Sat 10am–5pm
  Sunday 2pm–5pm
  Closed Monday
  Closed two weeks prior to Christmas

- **National Gallery**
  Telephone: (01) 661 5133
  Mon–Sat 10am–5.15pm
  (Thursday till 8.15pm)
  Sunday 2pm–5pm

- **Old Library and Book of Kells**
  Telephone: (01) 608 2308
  Mon–Sat 9.30am–5pm
  Sunday July–September:
  9.30am–4.30pm
  October–June: 12pm–4.30pm

- **House of Lords**
  Telephone: (01) 677 6801
  Mon–Fri 10am–4pm (Thursday till 5pm)

Hall. Cooley won the design competition over James Gandon's submission. (Gandon was later allowed to display his considerable talents as an architect when he designed, among other public buildings, the aforementioned Custom House and Four Courts.) The Corinthian portico and classical façade, the superbly executed rotunda (best viewed from inside the building), the urn-decorated ballustrade and the fine statues inside combine to make this one of Dublin's most important public buildings.

City Hall has been the location of significant historical events. It was requisitioned as a temporary military depot by the British authorities during the Irish rebellion of 1798, a rebellion which led to the Act of Union in 1800. This Act abolished the independent Irish Parliament and united it with the parliament in London. Other major events which took place here were the emotionally-charged funerals of Charles Stewart Parnell, Jeremiah O'Donovan Rossa and Michael Collins.

Cross over to City Hall from the pedestrian lights on the corner of Dame and Parliament Streets (beside Thomas Read's) and go up Cork Hill (not marked), named after the first Earl of Cork, whose home stood on the City Hall site, and take the first turn left. The side entrance into City Hall is to your left and the elegant, newly-restored façade of **Newcomen's Bank** is to your right. Newcomen's Bank was designed in 1781 by Thomas Ivory – the building is now used as offices of Dublin Corporation.

Go through the gates into the Upper Castle Yard of **Dublin Castle [67]**. (The gates are closed in the evening and on Saturday and Sunday mornings, in which case you should enter the Castle grounds through the lower gate, a hundred metres down the hill on the other side of City Hall.) The buildings surrounding the rectangular courtyard were mostly built between 1685 and 1760. The earlier sections were designed by Sir William Robinson (he also designed the Royal Hospital Kilmainham) and there have been major alterations over the intervening years. Directly opposite are the **State Apartments,** built as the residential quarters of the viceregal court. Visit, if you have the time.

Leave the courtyard through the archway on your left and descend into Lower Castle Yard. On your right is the **Chapel Royal**, designed by the Georgian architect Francis Johnston and built between 1807 and 1814. It was skilfully restored in 1989. The elaborate interior decorations include superb plasterwork by George Stapleton, wood carvings by Richard Stewart, and the arms of every Viceroy since 1172. Outside, there are over a hundred stone heads of historical characters by the celebrated sculptor Edward Smyth and his son.

At the bottom of the courtyard, turn left and go through the iron gates. Immediately on your left is the Sick and Indigent Roomkeepers' Society, founded in 1790 to provide relief for the city's poor. Go right, up the narrow and unkempt Dame Lane. Turn right at the end onto South Great George's Street and cross after a hundred metres to the far side, at the pedestrian crossing. Continue up South Great George's Street. The dominant, red-brick, Victorian block on your left is the South City Markets (1881). A much overlooked building, it was rebuilt in 1892 after a fire which destroyed much of the original. Go through Market Arcade (closed Sunday and Public Holidays), cross at the far end onto Castle Market, and walk to the end of this short pedestrianised street.

Directly ahead is **Powerscourt House**. Lord Powerscourt, whose principal residence was in County Wicklow, engaged the services of Robert Mack (architect of Grattan Bridge, starting point for this tour) to design a Dublin townhouse and, in 1774, the house was completed. Climb the granite steps leading to the front entrance and step into the front hall. As you proceed into the house, take time to admire the carved staircase, the extravagant plasterwork on the walls of the hall and stairway, and the exquisite plasterwork in the first floor reception rooms by Michael Stapleton. Walk through the entire complex – successfully converted in 1981 into a modern shopping mall – crossing as you go the covered courtyard (added in the early 1800s by Francis Johnston), and exit on the far side. Across the street on the left is the Carmelite church of St Teresa [**13**]. Go up the narrow laneway ahead – Johnston's Court – and at the end turn right onto Grafton Street.

Walk to the top of Grafton Street – explored in detail in *Around Grafton Street* – and cross towards the Fusiliers'Arch at the entrance to St Stephen's Green. Do not enter the park. Veer right and walk along St Stephen's Green West (the railings will be on your left). On your immediate right is the Stephen's Green Shopping Centre [**10**]. Pass on your left a statue by Jerome Connor of the patriot and revolutionary **Robert Emmet** (1778-1803), looking over towards his (demolished) birthplace at number 124 St Stephen's Green. He was executed outside St Catherine's Church on Thomas Street in 1803 at the age of 23, following a failed rebellion in Dublin.

As you proceed, the fine classical building on your right is the **Royal College of Surgeons**, a renowned medical college and one of the locations of the 1916 Easter Rising. Originally a three-bay pedimented building, architect William Murray added four more bays and re-centred the pediment in a major renovation between 1825 and 1827. A further addition in 1980 developed the entire complex down York Street, to the

left as you face the building. The College was occupied by a brigade of the Irish Volunteers during the 1916 Easter Rising: damage from British army firepower can be seen on the front stonework. Almost directly opposite the College of Surgeons is a seated statue of **Lord Ardilaun** (Arthur Edward Guinness) with his head inclined towards Guinness's Brewery at St James Gate: he was the proprietor from 1868 to 1877. It was Lord Ardilaun who bought, converted into public gardens and presented to the city the twenty-two acres which today is St Stephen's Green.

Continue to the corner and turn left and walk along the south side of the Green. The grey granite houses about one-third of the way along are numbers 85 and 86, collectively known as **Newman House**. Number 85, Clanwilliam House, was designed by German-born Richard Castle (formerly Cassels) in 1738 for a Member of Parliament, Captain Hugh Montgomery. It was probably the first stone-faced house on the Green. Its interior is an example of late baroque plasterwork at its most exquisite, the work of the celebrated Swiss stuccadores Paolo and Filippo Lafranchini. Visit, if you have the time. Number 86 was built for Richard 'Burn Chapel' Whaley MP in 1765 by Robert West and was decorated using the rococo style of plasterwork, executed by West himself.

Both houses were acquired in 1865 by the Catholic University of Ireland. The nineteenth-century writer and theologian John Henry Newman was its first rector and the houses were named after him. James Joyce attended college here between 1899 and 1902. Gerard Manley Hopkins was Professor of Classics between 1884 until his death in 1899. Others who studied here were the Dublin writer Brian O'Nolan (Flann O'Brien), and two leading figures in the 1916 Easter Rising, Patrick Pearse and Eamon de Valera.

Cross the street to the railings opposite and, before entering the park through the narrow gate directly ahead, look further along the Green to **Iveagh House**, the large, white building fifty metres along. It is home to the Department of Foreign Affairs and was donated to the State by Rupert Guinness, second Earl of Iveagh, in 1939. Previously it had been owned by Sir Benjamin Lee Guinness who had acquired the house in 1866. He transformed Richard Castle's 1736 building, changing the façade and adding a richly decorated ballroom. The original house had been commissioned as a town mansion for the Bishop of Cork and Ross, Robert Clayton and was probably Castle's first Dublin commission. None of the façade and only the first floor saloon of the original building remains.

Now, enter St Stephen's Green (explored in detail in *Three City Parks*). Immediately to your left is a bronze bust by Marjorie Fitzgibbon of James Joyce. Walk along the straight path directly ahead, past the bandstand on the left. Go through the central, circular section, and cross the small bridge over the lake (the other O'Connell Bridge in

Georgian door

Dublin). You are met by four paths – take the second on the left and exit the Green by the narrow gate thirty metres away. Go right and cross to Dawson Street at the lights.

Go down the right side of Dawson Street to the **Mansion House [9]**, a Queen Anne-style house, built in 1710, sold in 1715 to Dublin Corporation, and used as the official residence of the Lord Mayor of Dublin ever since. The Round Room, behind the main house, was designed by Francis Johnston and built in 1821, for the visit of King George IV.

Next down from the Mansion House is the **Royal Irish Academy [9]** and, next to it, **St Ann's Church [9]**, built in 1720 and retaining much of Isaac Wills' eighteenth-century interior. Extensive renovations carried out by Thomas Deane in 1868 changed the church's original exterior.

Take a right at European Union House and proceed up **Molesworth Street**. As you walk, note the two gable-style houses on the left, numbers 15 and 16 (built 1736) and further along on the far side, just past Buswell's Hotel, another house in the same style (built 1755). The houses were built by French Protestant Huguenots who had settled in Dublin and were known as 'Dutch Billies', after King William of Orange. Beside numbers 15 and 16 is **Masonic Hall**, home of the Grand Lodge of Freemasons in Ireland since 1865. Inside the sober nineteenth-century façade is a museum, and four unusual and quite distinct rooms, each designed in a different style: classical, ancient Egyptian, medieval Gothic and Tudor.

Walk to the end of the street. The trio of buildings directly opposite were once occupied by the Dublin Society, founded in 1731 to promote agriculture, the arts and science. It later became the Royal Dublin Society, is referred to as the RDS, and is now located in the nearby suburb of Ballsbridge. Cross to look at the Georgian mansion behind the central iron gates. This is **Leinster House**, designed by Richard Castle in 1745. He was commissioned by James Fitzgerald, Earl of Kildare, to design a large house on a vacant site southeast of Trinity College. Castle created a classical façade in his eleven-bay, forty-three metre-wide building, with a central pediment and Corinthian columns. When completed, Kildare House was the largest Georgian townhouse in Ireland. After the Earl was made Duke of Leinster in 1766, it was renamed Leinster

House. In 1922, the house was acquired by the Irish Free State Government and today is more commonly referred to as Dáil Éireann, the Irish Parliament. It houses An Dáil (Lower House), with 166 Members, and An Seanad (Senate), with 60 Senators.

To the left of Leinster House is the **National Library** and, to the right, the **National Museum**, both designed by Thomas Newenham Deane and his son between 1884 and 1890. The Library is a rich source of archive material, with newspapers, books, magazines, manuscripts, maps and photographs of historic and social interest available for consultation purposes. The Museum is an easy and enjoyable place to visit, being well laid out, not too cluttered and possessing an interesting display of artifacts from prehistoric times right up to the 1916 Easter Rising. There is a café in the building, so if you are craving a cup of tea and a scone, this could be the place for you.

Go right, up Kildare Street, past the Museum and passing on your right a wall plaque at number 30 marking the house in which Bram Stoker [112], author of Dracula, lived for a while. At the top of the street, turn left and walk past the Shelbourne Hotel [39], a fine Victorian building and among Dublin's most exclusive. After twenty metres, cross to the sculpted trio of arches and walk along St Stephen's Green East to the corner with Hume Street.

A confrontation took place here in 1969 involving conservationists and developers, the former who were trying to prevent some fine eighteenth-century corner houses from being demolished by the latter. They occupied the townhouses for six months before finally having to concede defeat. If you look closely, you will see who won 'the Battle of Hume Street', as it became known, for the corner houses here are poor imitations of the splendid originals.

Go up Hume Street. The fine, seven-bay Georgian townhouse, number 8 Ely Place, facing down Hume Street, was built for the Marquis of Ely, Henry Loftus, in 1771. It has superb plasterwork by Michael Stapleton but cannot be viewed as the house is not open to the public. Turn left into Ely Place and right at the lights into Baggot Street Lower. Pass two of Dublin's finest old pubs, Doheny & Nesbitt's [151] on your left and Toner's [151] on your right.

Go right into Pembroke Street Lower and walk to **Fitzwilliam Square** [102], the smallest, and last to be completed, of the five Georgian squares in the city. It was developed over a period of thirty-five years, between 1791 and 1825, its completion signalling the end of a unique period of building in Dublin which lasted almost one hundred years. It is the only Georgian square whose park is still reserved for residents. The houses around it are smaller than in the other four squares (Merrion, St Stephen's, Parnell and Mountjoy) but they are extremely well preserved. The doorways, which are painted in bright colours, are a particularly attractive feature. Traditionally, members of the legal profession were associated with the square,

Leinster House behind Leinster Lawn

but nowadays the medical profession are more in evidence.

Walk around three sides of the park – west, south, east – keeping the railings on your left. The third side you will walk along forms part of **Fitzwilliam Street**, a wide and long thoroughfare with Georgian townhouses on either side. This stretch, running from the top of the street behind you all the way down to where Holles Street Hospital closes the view in front of you, was once known as the Georgian Mile. At just over a half a mile, it was believed to have been the longest stretch of uninterrupted Georgian townhouse architecture in Europe.

Continue along Fitzwilliam Street and cross the intersection with Baggot Street Lower. The hundred-metre long office block on your right is the headquarters of the Electricity Supply Board (ESB), built in 1961. About twenty Georgian townhouses were demolished to make way for what you see today. Put simply, it was one of the worst acts of architectural state vandalism ever perpetuated and it lost Dublin its Georgian Mile title for ever.

In an effort to regain credibility, the ESB – assisted by the National Museum – restored **Number 29**

**49**

**Lower Fitzwilliam Street** – on the next corner on the right. This fine Georgian house, built in 1794 for a Mrs Olivia Beatty, has been decorated and furnished in the style of a typical Georgian townhouse of the period 1790-1820. You can visit the house – it's open to the public – and see at first hand how the Dublin upper classes lived at the end of the eighteenth century.

At this corner, look right, along Upper Mount Street to the graceful St Stephen's Church, usually referred to as the **Peppercannister Church [104]**. Turn left into Merrion Square South.

**Merrion Square [40]** was named in 1762 after the sixth Lord Fitzwilliam of Meryon and is generally thought of as the heart of Georgian Dublin. Built for the nobility and the gentry and laid out by architect John Ensor in the 1760s – the north and east sides being the first to be completed – the square is a magnificent showpiece for eighteenth-century townhouses. Note the houses' uniform height and use of

materials, the fine doorways with distinct, brass door knockers and letter boxes, the ornate, half-moon glass sunlights over the doors, the varied ironwork along many of the balconies, and the long windows of the first floor drawing-rooms in which guests were entertained in lavish parties during each Parliamentary term.

There are interesting wall plaques on many of the houses. Daniel O'Connell, the 'Liberator' and driving force behind the campaign for Catholic Emancipation, lived in number 58; the writer Joseph Sheridan le Fanu lived in number 70; William Butler Yeats lived for a time in number 82; and the poet, mystic and painter George Russell (AE) worked in number 84.

At this point, if you have the time, explore the interior of the square, referring to the *Three City Parks* tour on page 40.

Continue to the end of Merrion Square South. Across the wide Merrion Street Upper and to your left are the imposing **Government Buildings**, built between 1904 and 1922 for the Royal College of Science. They are now entirely in Government use, housing offices of Government ministers and of An Taoiseach, the Irish Prime Minister. Some years ago, under a former Taoiseach, Charles J. Haughey, an estimated £20 million was spent on restoring these buildings. Haughey, one of the most controversial politicians ever to hold office in Dáil Éireann, was keen on grandiose public projects, but a witty commentator, drawing on the fact that 'Chas' is sometimes used as an abbreviation

Campanile in Trinity College

of Charles, renamed this 'grand projet' *the Chas Mahal*.

Opposite the entrance to Government Buildings, number 24, also known as **Mornington House**, is believed to be the birthplace of Arthur Wellesley, Duke of Wellington, although the town of Trim in County Meath also lays claim to this fact. The house has been subsumed recently into a five-star hotel, incorporating a number of Georgian townhouses which had been lying idle and neglected for over a decade.

Cross Merrion Street Upper and stand at the railings of Leinster House. On your left is the Natural History Museum and beside it, **Leinster Lawn**. The obelisk in the centre of the lawn commemorates Michael Collins and Arthur Griffith, signatories to the 1921 Treaty between the Provisional Irish Government and the British Government, and also Kevin O'Higgins, the Irish Minister for Justice at the time. Behind the obelisk is Leinster House, seen earlier from Kildare Street.

Walk right, along the railings for fifty metres to the **National Gallery**, established by an Act of Parliament in 1854. A year earlier, the railway magnate William Dargan, whose statue stands on the Gallery lawn, had organised a huge, mainly industrial, exhibition on adjoining Leinster Lawn. Many of the paintings which were shown as part of that exhibition formed the nucleus of the early collection. Today, the Gallery has an impressive collection of paintings representing the major European schools, as well as a fine representative collection of Irish

painting. A statue of George Bernard Shaw, which until recently stood near Dargan, now stands in the Dargan Wing (the large exhibition room on the left as you enter). Shaw left a significant proportion of his estate to the National Gallery.

Directly across the street at this point is the Rutland Fountain, designed in 1791 to commemorate the Duke of Rutland, a former Viceroy, and his wife. It has been recently restored.

Continue to the traffic lights. On the diagonally opposite corner is the American College in Dublin, housed in **number 1 Merrion Square**, one of Dublin's best-known literary addresses, for it was here that Oscar Wilde lived with his larger-than-life parents, Sir William and Lady (Speranza) Wilde [**114**]. The oldest and most impressive houses on Merrion Square are on this side of Merrion Square, some of them dating from 1764.

Turn left into Clare Street and pass Greene's Bookshop, with its lovely old shopfront, on your way to Nassau Street. Across Nassau Street are the railings of Trinity College, behind which are the grounds of College Park. Staying on the left, walk for a couple of hundred metres to where Kildare Street (visited earlier) goes left at the traffic lights. On this corner is the now defunct **Kildare Street Club**, shared today by the Alliance Française and the State Heraldic Museum. Built between 1858 and 1861, and designed by Benjamin Woodward and Thomas Deane, this is one of Dublin's more interesting Victorian buildings, notwithstanding the battering it has received over the years from adverse weather, urban pollution and insensitive restructuring in 1971 which carved up the splendid interior and destroyed a magnificent staircase. Look closely at the base of the exterior columns and you will see the partly eroded outline of carved monkeys playing snooker, a greyhound chasing a hare and a bear playing a violin. These stone carvings are the work of the O'Shea brothers, who were much sought after on account of the quality of their stone work.

Continue for 250 m and cross Nassau Street at the corner of Dawson Street (beside the Ulster Bank) and enter **Trinity College**. The college was established by Queen Elizabeth I in 1592 and is the oldest university in Ireland. It was situated east of the medieval, walled city, and occupied a site on which had stood the Augustinian Priory of All Hallows, founded by Dermot MacMurrough of Leinster.

The covered passageway you are walking along cuts through the modern Arts and Social Science Building and leads to Fellows' Square. The Old Library faces you across the square. Also referred to as the Long Room Library, it was designed by Thomas Burgh and built between 1712 and 1732. The library itself, at sixty-four metres in length and with a barrel-vaulted oak ceiling (added in 1859), is a magnificent achievement and worth seeing, even if the building didn't also happen to house the Book of Kells, the Book of Armagh and the Book of Durrow, together with Ireland's most

important collection of books, manuscripts and historical documents.

Stay on the left of Fellows' Square and walk past the unusual Reading Room on your left and into Parliament (or Front) Square. Directly ahead of you is the College Campanile, or Bell Tower, standing between Parliament and Library Square and built in 1852, replacing an original designed by Richard Castle. The two symmetrical buildings facing each other across Parliament Square are, across the courtyard, the College Chapel (1798) and, on your immediate left, the Examination Hall (1785), both designed by Sir William Chambers towards the end of the eighteenth century and the last of the great Georgian buildings to be built in the College. Both have low-slung, barrel-vaulted ceilings, with superb plasterwork by Michael Stapleton. The Examination Hall, usually out of bounds to visitors, has a magnificent oak chandelier which formerly hung in the old Irish House of Commons, now the main banking chamber of the Bank of Ireland on College Green. The Chapel, shared by all Christian denominations, is frequently open.

Beside the Chapel and set back from the square is the Dining Hall. The original building was designed by Richard Castle in 1743 but there were major construction difficulties and the re-designed building, by Hugh Darley, wasn't completed until 1758. Following a fire, which gutted the building in 1984, the present building, replicating the original, was built.

No buildings remain from the Elizabethan foundation. Trinity's oldest building, the student residential Rubrics (red brick), at the end of Library Square, were built in 1700 but have been much altered since. Other important buildings to see are the splendid Venetian Gothic Museum Building, designed by Thomas Deane and Benjamin Woodward in 1854. (To fully appreciate it, you will need to walk to the back of the Rubrics where you can view it from New Square); and Richard Castle's miniature Printing House (also behind the Rubrics), designed as a Doric temple in 1734.

Exit the college through the front arch, at the western end of Parliament Square (between the Chapel and the Examination Hall). The noise of College Green will give you a jolt, after the tranquillity within the college grounds. Statues of Oliver Goldsmith and Edmund Burke stand inside the railings, facing up Dame Street. Behind them is the ninety-metre classical façade of the college, built between 1752 and 1759.

Cross to the pedestrian island directly ahead, on College Green. The **Bank of Ireland** dominates the scene. Built between 1729 and 1739 as the House of Parliament, it was designed by Edward Lovett Pearce, with later additions east and west of the original portico by the architects James Gandon and Robert Parke, respectively. It is one of the finest public buildings in Dublin and was the first building in the world designed to be a two-chamber legislature. During its period as the Irish Parliament, it was the envy of most parliaments throughout Europe. Its sheer size dwarfed every other building in the city.

After power was removed from the Irish Parliament by the Act of Union in 1800 (actually, the Parliament voted itself out of existence, a scenario difficult to envisage in any present-day parliament *anywhere*), the Bank of Ireland bought the building for £40,000 and they immediately engaged the Georgian architect Francis Johnston to convert it to banking use. In the alterations, the House of Commons was altered beyond recognition, as was much of the interior.

In an unusual move, the bank's owners decided to retain the House of Lords in its original splendour. It is open to the public during banking hours and there are tours which, if you have the time and the energy by this stage of the tour, are free, informative and entertaining.

The Palladian central block, facing south (and you) around which stand monumental Ionic columns, is topped by Royal Arms in the tympanum, and statues of Fidelity on the left, Hibernian in the middle and Commerce on the right. The Corinthian columns at the House of Lords portico are adorned with statues of Fortitude, Justice and Liberty.

Your tour ends here, in the centre of the city. Beside you is Temple Bar, with dozens of possibilities for a refreshing drink, a light meal or a four-course dinner. Relax – you've earned it!

Most guidebooks concentrate on the south inner city when referring to Georgian Dublin. This tour redresses the imbalance. Two of the five Georgian squares in Dublin are on the north side of the Liffey; the two most impressive of all eighteenth-century public buildings are situated along the north Liffey quays; the most spectacular rococo plasterwork interior in all of Dublin is in the Rotunda Chapel at the northern end of O'Connell Street; and the faded elegance of North Great George's Street and Henrietta Street surpass anything the south inner city can offer. The tour can be completed, at a leisurely pace, in a morning or an afternoon, or, you can make a pleasant day of it, stopping for lunch along the way.

**Tour begins:** *on George's Quay, beside Tara Street DART and Train Station.*

Stand on George's Quay and look across the River Liffey at the **Custom House** (1781-91), widely regarded as Dublin's finest eighteenth-century public building. It provides a reminder, to all who see and admire it, of the importance of Dublin as a trading port and as an economic centre of activity in the late 1700s. Only a thriving and confident city and one with a real sense of its place in the world would consider building such a magnificent edifice, against all the odds and against the expressed wish – sometimes violently – of many of Dublin's traders at the time.

James Gandon, arguably the most accomplished architect ever to work in Dublin, was frequently seen on the construction site of the Custom House carrying a sword, such was the building's extreme unpopularity. Local residents feared the area would become a slum, while merchants and traders in the Temple Bar area of the city – where the existing Custom House stood – feared for their livelihood.

## Tour Facts

- **Length of tour:** 4.5 miles (7.2 kilometres)
- **Duration of tour:** a leisurely 2 hours
- **Refreshments:** during the tour (Dublin Writers Museum Café; Municipal Gallery Café); after the tour (the Brazen Head; any of the quayside cafés on your walk back towards O'Connell Bridge)
- **Getting to the Starting Point:** from O'Connell Bridge, walk down Burgh Quay until you reach Tara Street DART Station and George's Quay
- **Special Note for Walkers:** There are some neglected areas along the route. While it is quite safe – taking the usual precautions – to do the tour in daylight hours, it is not advisable to undertake the tour after dark

In fact, the new building transformed the dynamic of the city because, only a few years after its completion, Carlisle (now O'Connell) Bridge was built and the city's axis shifted eastwards.

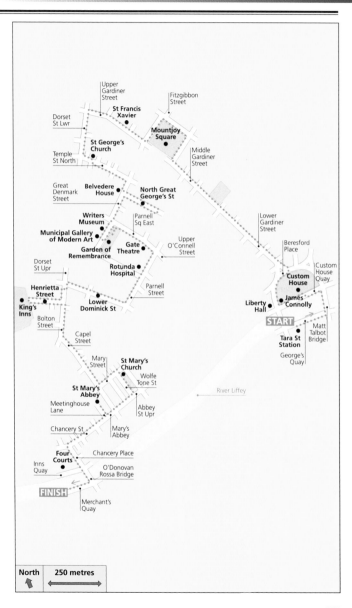

Upper
Gardiner
Street

Fitzgibbon
Street

**St Francis
Xavier**

Dorset
St Lwr

**Mountjoy
Square**

**St George's
Church**

Temple
St North

Middle
Gardiner
Street

Great
Denmark
Street

**Belvedere
House**

**North Great
George's St**

**Writers
Museum**

Parnell
Sq East

Lower
Gardiner
Street

**Municipal Gallery
of Modern Art**

Upper
O'Connell
Street

Beresford
Place

**Garden of
Remembrance**

**Gate
Theatre**

Custom
House
Quay

Dorset
St Upr

**Rotunda
Hospital**

**Custom
House**

**Henrietta
Street**

Parnell
Street

**Liberty
Hall**

**James
Connolly**

**King's
Inns**

**Lower
Dominick St**

Bolton
Street

**START**

Capel
Street

**Tara St
Station**

Matt
Talbot
Bridge

Mary
Street

**St Mary's
Church**

George's
Quay

Wolfe
Tone St

**St Mary's
Abbey**

River Liffey

Meetinghouse
Lane

Abbey
St Upr

Chancery St

Mary's
Abbey

**Four
Courts**

Chancery Place

Inns
Quay

O'Donovan
Rossa Bridge

**FINISH**

Merchant's
Quay

North

250 metres

## Opening Times

- **James Joyce Cultural Centre**
  Telephone (01) 878 8547
  June–August
  Mon–Sat  9.30am–5pm
  Sunday and Holidays
  11am–5pm
  September–May
  Mon–Sat  9.30am–5pm
  Sunday and Holidays
  12.30pm–5pm
- **Dublin Writers Museum**
  Telephone (01) 872 2077
  Mon–Sat  10am–5pm
  Sunday and Holidays
  11am–5pm
  Late opening Mon–Fri  till 6pm
  in June, July and August
- **Hugh Lane Municipal Gallery of Modern Art**
  Telephone (01) 874 1903
  Tues–Thurs  9.30am–6pm
  Friday and Saturday
  9.30am–5pm
  Sunday 11am–5pm
  Closed Monday
- **Rotunda Hospital Chapel**
  Telephone (01) 873 0700
  Telephone for details
- **St Mary's Abbey Chapter House**
  Mid-June–Mid-September
  Sunday and Wednesday
  10am–5pm

The building dominates the eastern Liffey quays. To the nineteenth-century sea merchants arriving into Dublin for the first time, it must have been an inspiring sight. The building is 114 metres long, with a central Corinthian column and arcades on each side linking the end pavilions. The splendid statues and stone carvings are by Edward Smyth and are probably this prolific sculptor's best work. The four statues on the roof represent Neptune, Mercury, Plenty and Industry. The central column is topped by a copper dome above which stands a towering figure representing Hope.

In 1921 the entire building was gutted by a fire during a skirmish in the War of Independence, but it was later rebuilt with complete fidelity to the original. The Custom House has been the home of different Government departments since the 1920s and today houses the Department of the Environment.

Walk to the eastern end (towards the sea) of George's Quay and cross the Liffey at Matt Talbot Bridge, named after the Venerable Matt Talbot [132]. Turn left and walk along Custom House Quay to admire the Custom House at close quarters. Exercising caution, cross to the Custom House side and continue around the corner and stop at Eamonn O'Doherty's statue of **James Connolly**. Connolly founded the modern labour movement and is seen here with the Starry Plough, the flag of the Irish Citizen Army, founded in 1913 as a workers' defence force. Across the street is **Liberty Hall**, Dublin's tallest building and headquarters of the Irish trade union movement. It was from a building on the site of Liberty Hall that Connolly led members of the Irish Citizen Army and the Irish Volunteers to the General Post Office on Easter Monday morning, 1916, from the steps of which Patrick Pearse and his co-revolutionaries read out the Proclamation of Independence.

Continue walking around the

Custom House for about 150 m and stop at the traffic lights. Directly ahead is one of the prominent modern buildings in what is officially called the **Irish Financial Services Centre**, in which more than 200 international financial institutions operate. In the same direction but to the left is the central bus terminus, **Busarus**, built in 1953 by architect Michael Scott in what was an adventurous departure from the architectural norm at the time. Almost half a century later, it looks dated and dull. Between the two, on the traffic island, is an inspiring sculpture commemorating the work of **Amnesty International**. An eternal flame reminds passersby of the many thousand prisoners of conscience held captive across the globe. Before crossing to Lower Gardiner Street, look at the curved Georgian terrace facing this northern section of the Custom House. It was from here, **Beresford Place,** and from neighbouring Gardiner Street, that much of the local objection to the building of the Custom House emanated.

Walk along the right side of Lower Gardiner Street. This area, including Beresford Place, was laid out and developed by the forward-thinking and energetic eighteenth-century developer Luke Gardiner. Today, Gardiner Street is one of the principal tourist accommodation districts in Dublin, many of the large Georgian townhouses finding their saviour in tourism. For a time, it looked as if most of Gardiner Street would go the way of the upper end of the street, where dilapidated houses were allowed to become derelict and were finally

demolished to make way for modern, non descript apartment blocks. Fortunately, much of this lower part has survived intact. Walk all the way up Gardiner Street. This is one of the least interesting parts of the walk, so don't hang about. At the brow of the hill, turn right into Mountjoy Square South.

**Mountjoy Square** is one of two eighteenth-century squares on the north side of the city. It was developed between 1792 and 1818 and for a time was called Gardiner Square, after Luke Gardiner, who later in life became Viscount Mountjoy. It was one of the most fashionable districts in the city, however you don't have to look too closely to see the signs of neglect today. Fortunately, the Celtic Tiger (the name given to Ireland's economic resurgence) seems to have stopped the rot. *Unfortunately*, the renewal comes far too late for many of the houses, especially those which lined the southern and western sides. Their neglect over the years resulted inevitably in demolition, making way for pastiche replacements in many cases. The playwright Seán O'Casey lived at number 35 (original house demolished) and his fine play, *The Shadow of a Gunman*, is probably set here. Brian Boru is believed to have camped in the area during the Battle of Clontarf in 1014.

Walk around three sides – south, east and north – keeping the railings of the park on your left. An odd fact is that Mountjoy Square is the only actual square square (!) among Dublin's five Georgian squares – the others are all rectangles despite being called squares. At right angles to the

Custom House at night

north-eastern corner runs Fitzgibbon Street: James Joyce spent some of his boyhood at number 14. When you complete the northern side, turn right into Gardiner Street Upper and walk to the Catholic church of **St Francis Xavier**, built between 1829 and 1832 and housing a splendid Italian high altar and a beautifully decorated coffered ceiling. The church is featured at the end of James Joyce's short story, *Grace*.

*'A powerful-looking figure, the upper part of which was draped with a white surplice, was observed to be struggling up into the pulpit. Simultaneously the congregation unsettled, produced handkerchiefs and knelt upon them with care.'*

Continue past the church and turn left into Dorset Street. There is nothing of interest to see along here, so proceed without delay and take the second left into Temple Street and walk to **St George's Church** on Hardwicke Place. Cross to the far side to view it properly. Designed by Francis Johnston in 1802, many regard it as the Georgian architect's finest work, although it is impossible to appreciate it fully as it is no longer in use as a church (it was

deconsecrated in 1990 and converted in the mid-nineties into the Temple Theatre). One can still admire the building's façade and the rising spire which was modelled on St Martin-in-the-Fields. The top of the spire is almost 200 feet from the ground. Inside, there is a wonderful feeling of space, and the stained glass windows by Evie Hone are especially fine. The church bells were added in 1836 after neighbours of Johnston, who lived in nearby Eccles Street, complained about the noise they made; Johnston, a lover of bells, had had them installed in a purpose-built bell-tower in his back garden! He gave his neighbours a break – not to mention a night's sleep – when he donated the bells to St George's. The Duke of Wellington was married in this church.

Continue along Temple Street, past the Children's Hospital, and turn right at the end into Great Denmark Street. The large house on the right about fifty metres along, with the seven granite steps leading up to the Georgian door, is **Belvedere House**, built in the mid 1770s for the second Lord Belvedere. It has been a Jesuit school for boys – Belvedere College – since 1841. The new owners left intact the beautiful Apollo and Diana Rooms, which have marvellous plasterwork by Michael Stapleton. Regrettably, the central part of Stapleton's ceiling in the Venus Room was removed in 1841. The fireplaces, by the Venetian, Bossi, are among the finest in Dublin. James Joyce attended school here 1893-8, and it is featured in his *Portrait of the Artist as a Young Man.* Belvedere College is not open to the public.

Directly opposite the college is **North Great George's Street**, dating from around 1775 and which, remarkably, has survived the urban decay which beset much of north Dublin's eighteenth-century building stock. Walk down the left side of the street, as far as the James Joyce Cultural Centre at number 35, and return along the right side. During the early nineteenth century, there was a large iron gate at the bottom of the street and this, mirrored at the other end by Belvedere House, gave the street a private and exclusive air. The past decade has seen quite a transformation in the condition of most of the houses. Committed conservationists, among them the Joycean scholar Senator David Norris, who has a house here, have taken the street by the scruff of the neck and have slowly been bringing it back to life. Norris has also been a leading force in the development of the **James Joyce Cultural Centre [119]**.

Back on Great Denmark Street, turn left and continue to the end. Cross to the neo-Gothic Abbey Presbyterian Church, better known as '**Findlater's Church**'. Built in 1864 with money provided by a wealthy, Scottish-born brewer and grocer, Alex Findlater, it has one of the city's most striking church steeples.

A few doors along, at number 18 Parnell Square, is the **Dublin Writers Museum**, housing collections of rare editions, manuscript items and memorabilia relating to a long list of Irish writers, all in an eighteenth-century townhouse setting. There is also a library of rare books, a gallery of portraits and busts, a bookshop and a café.

Continue to the **Hugh Lane Municipal Gallery of Modern Art**, originally Charlemont House and designed by Sir William Chambers (he also designed the Chapel and Examination Hall in Trinity College) between 1762 and 1765 for the Earl of Charlemont. The Earl was a wealthy member of the aristocracy who, at the age of nineteen, went travelling for six months in Europe and stayed nine years! Upon his return, weighed down with works of art from Continental Europe, he set about establishing himself in the capital. His country mansion, on the northern outskirts of the city, has been carefully restored and is now a national monument and a national architectural treasure. It is called the Casino in Marino.

The building you are looking at on Parnell Square scarcely resembles the splendid Georgian mansion of 1765, such have been the extensive modifications over the years. In 1927, the Irish Government presented the house to the city and Dublin Corporation undertook the renovation, adapting the interior for use as an art gallery. The Hugh Lane Municipal Gallery of Modern Art was opened in 1933, named after the man who was a patron of the arts until he died in the 1915 sinking of the Lusitania. An agreement between the London Tate Gallery and the Municipal Gallery, made in 1994 and due to expire around 2008, decrees that twenty-seven of the Hugh Lane Bequest paintings remain on loan in Dublin, while a

**59**

further eight will move between the National Gallery in London and Dublin.

Cross the street – take extreme care, as the cars can sometimes appear out of nowhere from your right – and walk back the way you came and enter the **Garden of Remembrance**, opened in 1966 to commemorate the fiftieth anniversary of the 1916 Easter Rising. The unusual and striking sculpture represents the *Children of Lir* [**121**] who, according to legend, were turned into swans for 900 years. It was executed by Oisín Kelly.

On leaving the Garden, turn right and walk down Parnell Square East towards O'Connell Street. **Parnell Square** was the second Georgian square to be laid out, after St Stephen's Green. Originally Rutland Square, the northern terrace was laid out in 1755. During its development, the altruistic and charitable Bartholomew Mosse was putting into motion his plans for the building of a maternity hospital on the south, or lower, side of the square. This was to become known as Dr Mosse's Lying-In Hospital, now the Rotunda. To raise money, Mosse converted the grounds behind the hospital into the most elegant of private gardens into which Lords, Ladies, Dukes, Earls and Members of Parliament flocked, transforming the **Rotunda Gardens** into an aristocratic amusement ground and Rutland Square into one of the most fashionable areas of the city. By 1792, Rutland Square was home to eleven peers, two bishops and eleven members of Parliament.

On your left as you descend is number 5, where Oliver St John Gogarty, a contemporary of James Joyce and prototype for the character Buck Mulligan in the opening passage of *Ulysses*, was born in 1878. On your right is the **Gate Theatre**, founded in 1928 and occupying the 1786 New Assembly Rooms, built by Bartholomew Mosse in his bid to raise money for his hospital. Immediately beyond the entrance to the theatre is an old horse trough, an item of Dublin street furniture very common throughout the city as recently as the 1950s.

At the bottom of the hill, you have a fine view along O'Connell Street and, in the foreground, the impressive Parnell Monument [**22**]. Turn right into Parnell Street. The Ambassador Cinema, on your immediate right, was built as the **Rotunda Room** in 1766 by Bartholomew Mosse and later improved by James Gandon. Beyond the Ambassador is the Rotunda Hospital itself, with the dome of the **Rotunda Chapel** immediately on your right, behind the railings. The rococo decoration in the chapel, executed by Bartholomew Cramillion, is without question one of the most remarkable interiors in Dublin. Completed in 1758, the chapel is for residents and visitors only, however it may be worth your while to seek permission to visit. The entrance to the hospital is around the next corner.

The **Rotunda Hospital** is allegedly the oldest maternity hospital in the world. Founded by Bartholomew Mosse on 15 March 1745 in George's Lane, now South Great George's Street, and opposite Fade Street, the small hospital achieved such a reputation that, by 1750, Mosse commissioned his friend and architect Richard Castle to design a large hospital here. Castle, aware of Mosse's financial constraints, used his earlier Leinster House design as the blueprint for the new building. By 1757, the magnificent Lying-In Hospital had opened its doors, doors which were principally used by the poverty-stricken pregnant women of Dublin.

Continue past the hospital and proceed along Parnell Street. Moore Street, with its street traders, is on your left. After a couple of hundred metres, turn right into **Lower Dominick Street**, one of the most fashionable streets in Dublin in the eighteenth and nineteenth centuries. Today it is a mere shadow of its former glory, all the houses at the Parnell Street end having been demolished during the 1950s and 60s and replaced by the uninspired Dublin Corporation flats you see today. One of the most remarkable of all the remaining Georgian townhouses in Dublin did survive, however. The house, **number twenty**, on the right, directly opposite Dominick Lane, was built by the celebrated builder and stuccodore Robert West in 1753. West went to town on his stucco work in this, his own house, plastering the walls and ceilings with some of the most elaborate decorations imaginable. And, while the extravagant high relief stucco style may not be to everyone's personal taste, it is undeniably impressive and a rich example of native Irish stucco

work. The house is not open to the public, however if you feel you simply must see the interior, you can make enquiries at the nearby St Saviour's Orphanage.

King's Inns

The other building of note on the street is **St Saviour's Church** (1861), the most important of the many churches designed by the Dublin-born architect James Joseph McCarthy. Some of the street's past inhabitants include the mathematician Sir William Rowan Hamilton, born at number 36 (demolished); the novelist Joseph Sheridan le Fanu, born at number 45 (demolished); the Dukes of Leinster who, for a time during the nineteenth century, lived at number 13 (demolished); and the playwright Seán O'Casey, who lived above St Mary's School for a time.

Turn left just past the church into Bolton Street. Cross – carefully – and go right, up **Henrietta Street**, a hundred metres down. Developed by Luke Gardiner in the 1720s (he lived in number 10), Henrietta Street was the earliest of the important Georgian streets to be built in Dublin. In its early years, it was known as Primate's Hill because of the many senior clergy and at least one archbishop who lived here. By the time of the Act of Union in 1800, many of the houses were occupied by the aristocracy. By the middle of the nineteenth century, the aristocracy had been replaced by the legal profession and by the end of that century these in turn had been replaced by the poor, living in what had become squalid slums. Some of the larger houses were sub-divided into fifteen to twenty individual tenements, with poverty-stricken families living in each one. The street has never recovered from that period and has, incredibly for a city which boasts its Georgian heritage, been ignored in terms of conservation or restoration schemes. A convent occupies the well-preserved numbers 8 to 10, at the top of the street. Edward Lovett Pearce (chief architect of the old House of Parliament, now the Bank of Ireland, on College Green) designed numbers 9 and 10.

The **King's Inns**, at the top of the street, is the home of the legal profession. The building was designed by James Gandon and was begun in 1795, however it took until 1817 to complete, by which time other architects had become involved, among them Francis Johnston, who designed the triumphal arch. Go through the passageway to view the building from the Constitution Hill side. The interior of the building is not easily seen as its use is for members of the King's Inns only.

Go back down Henrietta Street, passing on the right the home of *Na Piobairi Uilleann* (the Piper's Club) at number 15, where classes in traditional musical instrument playing as well as in set dancing are given throughout the year. Turn right into Bolton Street and cross – again, very carefully – to the far side, passing the imposing Bolton Street College of Technology before veering left at the fork into Capel Street. At the next fork in the road, approximately a hundred metres along, keep right and walk about half the length of Capel Street. You can see as far as the Royal Exchange (now City Hall) at the southern end of Parliament Street, across the Liffey.

Turn left into Mary Street. **St Mary's Church** is about one hundred metres along on the right, at the corner of Mary Street and Wolfe Tone Street. The design of St Mary's is attributed to the architect of the Long Room Library in Trinity College, Thomas Burgh. It is one of the city's oldest churches, having been completed in 1702. During the eighteenth century it was Dublin's most fashionable church. Arthur Guinness married Ann Lee here in 1793, and a host of famous Irishmen were baptised here, among them the Earl of Charlemont in 1728, the writer Richard Brinsley Sheridan in 1751, the patriot Theobald Wolfe Tone in 1763 (he was born in Wolfe Tone Street), the mathematician Sir William Rowan Hamilton in 1805, and the playwright Seán O'Casey in 1880.

St Mary's has gone the way of many Protestant churches in the city, having been converted for use as a retail outlet and, more recently, being resurrected as a pub and a restaurant. It seems that one religion – commerce – has replaced the real thing in some parts of the city. It is hard not to feel angry – and sad – that such an important church was neglected for so long and is now reduced to serving food and drink.

Turn right and walk along Wolfe Tone Street, passing on your left Wolfe Tone Park, formerly the church's cemetery. Turn right at the next junction into Abbey Street Upper and, when you reach Capel Street, continue in a straight line into Mary's Abbey. After fifty metres, turn right into Meetinghouse Lane, where are situated the chapter-house remains of the twelfth-century Cistercian **St Mary's Abbey**, one of the most important monasteries in Ireland up until its dissolution in 1537 by Henry VIII.

Continue along Mary's Abbey, passing as you go the Dublin Corporation Fruit and Vegetable markets on your right. After a few hundred metres, you will see the Four Courts, with its copper-green dome, ahead on your left. At Hughes pub, turn left and walk along Chancery Place to Inns Quay. To properly view the Four Courts, I suggest you cross the Liffey and turn right onto Merchant's Quay. Lean on the quayside wall anywhere along here and allow your eyes to rest on the magnificent Georgian building across the river.

The **Four Courts**, home of the Irish Law Courts, were designed by James Gandon and begun in 1786, though the building was not completed until 1802. This was partly because Gandon, fearing civil strife towards the end of the century, returned to England for a period. The building comprises a large, pedimented central Corinthian block, topped with a colonnaded rotunda and dome and joined on each side by a courtyard with open arcades facing onto the quayside. These courtyards are joined by two end-pavilions. The entire façade stretches along Inns Quay for about 130 metres. The five statues on the central pediment are by Edward Smyth, and represent Moses, Justice, Mercy, Wisdom and Authority.

The building was badly damaged in 1922 when anti-Treaty forces, which had taken up occupation, were fired on by the Free State Government from Merchant's Quay, under the command of Michael Collins. In the ensuing fire which engulfed the building, irreplaceable historical records were lost from the Public Records Office. The present building, rebuilt in 1932, remained true to Gandon's original and is considered by some to be Dublin's finest eighteenth-century public building. The western (upriver) section is part of an earlier design by Thomas Cooley, who had defeated Gandon in an architectural competition to design the Royal Exchange.

The Four Courts stands on the former site of a 1224 Dominican foundation, the Abbey of St Saviour. Stones from this demolished abbey were used to build two of old Dublin's fortified stone gates, St Audoen's Gate and Winetavern Street Gate. Some of these stones are today in the wall around St Audoen's Gate on Cook Street [**74**].

This is where your tour ends. You are only a few hundred metres from Dublin's oldest pub, The Brazen Head [**147**] (at the far end of Merchant's Quay turn left up Lower Bridge Street and the pub is on the right).

# ☩ Walk Back In Time

## A walking tour of Viking and Medieval Dublin

A fascinating trip back in time, to when the Vikings descended on the island's eastern shores and changed the course of history. A thousand years later, few Viking or Medieval remains can be seen *in situ*; most are long since buried, destroyed or recycled back into the city's built fabric.

During the tour, you will see where the Vikings first landed and where they first founded the 'old city'. You will have an opportunity to visit some of the city's most magnificent buildings, most notably Dublin Castle and the two medieval cathedrals of St Patrick and Christ Church.

The tour can be completed in a leisurely morning or afternoon amble, without visits. If you intend visiting the cathedrals and the Castle, plan for a full day.

### Tour Facts

- **Length:** 3.6 miles (5.8 kilometres)
- **Duration:** a leisurely 2 hours
- **Refreshments:** during the tour (Leo Burdock's Fish and Chip Shop on Werburgh Street; the Brazen Head pub on Lower Bridge Street); after the tour (multiple choice, I'll leave it to you)
- **Getting to the Starting Point:** from Trinity front gates (walk right, along the railings for 300 m and cross to the left at the pedestrian lights); from O'Connell Bridge (walk down Burgh Quay, take the first right, walk to the end and you will see the Steyne Monument directly ahead)

 **Tour begins:** *at the Steyne Monument on College Street, opposite the Screen Cinema.*

The erection of a stone monolith, or steyne, was common procedure by the Vikings and usually marked the location of their first berthing. The original steyne was erected by the Vikings in the early part of the ninth century and stood at this spot until its removal in 1726. The **Steyne Monument** is a 13-foot-high stone slab by Cliodna Cussen and was erected in 1984. It is surrounded by a small, landscaped garden. The entire area around here was submerged by the River Liffey at the time the Vikings sailed in from the bay.

From here, cross to the Trinity side of College Street and walk the few hundred metres to the front gates of the college. **Trinity College [52]** was founded in 1592 on the site of **All Hallows Priory**, an Augustinian establishment founded by the King of Leinster, Dermot MacMurrough, in 1166. The Priory almost certainly replaced an even earlier religious settlement. Indeed, it is possible that the first visual evidence of human settlement seen by the

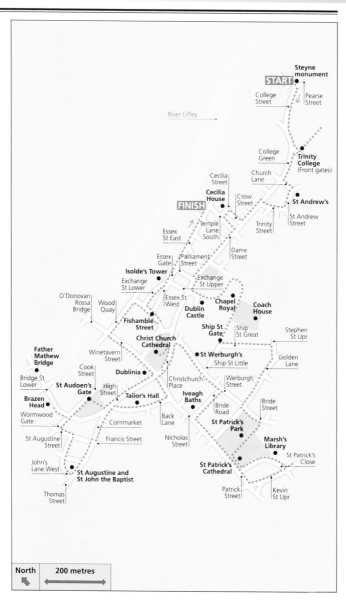

START
Steyne monument
College Street
Pearse Street
River Liffey
College Green
Trinity College (Front gates)
Church Lane
Cecilia Street
Cecilia House
Crow Street
St Andrew's
FINISH
Temple Lane South
St Andrew Street
Essex St East
Parliament Street
Trinity Street
Dame Street
Essex Gate
Isolde's Tower
Exchange St Lower
Exchange St Upper
O'Donovan Rossa Bridge
Wood Quay
Essex St West
Dublin Castle
Chapel Royal
Coach House
Fishamble Street
Ship St Gate
Ship St Great
Stephen St Upr
Christ Church Cathedral
St Werburgh's
Golden Lane
Father Mathew Bridge
Winetavern Street
Ship St Little
Cook Street
Dublinia
Christchurch Place
Werburgh Street
Bridge St Lower
St Audoen's Gate
High Street
Tailor's Hall
Iveagh Baths
Bride Road
Bride Street
Brazen Head
Wormwood Gate
Cornmarket
Back Lane
St Patrick's Park
St Augustine Street
Francis Street
Nicholas Street
Marsh's Library
John's Lane West
St Augustine and St John the Baptist
St Patrick's Close
Thomas Street
St Patrick's Cathedral
Patrick Street
Kevin St Upr

North
200 metres

## Opening Times

- **Chapel Royal and Record Tower**
  Telephone (01) 677 7129
  Mon–Fri 10am–12.45pm,
  2pm–5pm
  Sat/Sun/Bank Holidays:
  2pm–5pm
- **St Patrick's Cathedral**
  Telephone (01) 475 4817
  Mon–Fri 9am–6pm
  Saturday 9am–5pm
  Sunday April–September:
  9.30am–11am; 12.45pm–3pm;
  4.15pm–5pm
  October–March: 10am–11am;
  12.45pm–3pm
- **Marsh's Library**
  Telephone (01) 454 3511
  Monday and Wed–Fri
  10am–12.45pm; 2pm–5pm
  Saturday 10.30am–12.45pm
  Closed Tuesday and Sunday
- **St Werburgh's Church**
  Telephone: (01) 478 3710
  Mon–Fri 10am–4pm, by
  appointment only
  Sunday morning service at 10am
- **Christ Church Cathedral**
  Telephone: (01) 677 8099
  Daily 9.30am–5pm
- **Dublinia**
  Telephone: (01) 679 4611
  April–September
  Daily 10am–5pm
  October–March
  Mon–Sat 11am–4pm
  Sunday 10am–4.30pm
- **Dublin's Viking Adventure**
  Telephone (01) 679 6040
  Tues–Sat 10am–4.30pm (tours
  every half-hour)
  Closed Sunday and Monday

Vikings as they sailed into the River Liffey inlet was the steeple of this monastic settlement.

Briefly, go through the two arches into Parliament Square. Directly ahead is the College Campanile, or bell tower. The Campanile stands on what is believed to be the approximate site of All Hallows. Future excavations may confirm its exact location.

Return to the main gates of the College. In front of you is College Green, known in medieval times as **Hoggen Green**, an area of common pasture until the seventeenth century. The name Hoggen, which remained in use until 1666, derives from the Scandinavian word for a mound, *hogges*. Here, it almost certainly relates to a series of prehistoric burial mounds in this area.

From Trinity gates, cross to the left side of College Green and walk away from Trinity. As you proceed, look right, to the magnificent Bank of Ireland [**53**], a monumental building by any standards. Turn left at the Ulster Bank and walk up the short and narrow Church Lane, at the top of which is the Protestant church of St Andrew, now the main tourist information centre in Dublin. In Viking times, a forty-foot mound occupied the site of the church and was known as the **Thingmote**. It was used by the Viking authorities as their place of parliament. Here, laws were enacted, decrees were made, and punishments were handed out. Some of these, such as executions, were carried out below, on Hoggen Green.

Go past St Andrew Street Post Office (opposite the church) and

# Walk Back In Time

turn right, into Trinity Street. At College Green, cross to the far side at the pedestrian lights beside the Pen Shop, going left when you step on the far pavement. You are now on Dame Street. Go past the Central Bank [26] and Fownes Street, turn right and walk down Crow Street. Directly ahead, at the bottom of the street, is **Cecilia House** [27], formerly the Catholic University School of Medicine, and built on the site of an important Augustinian Friary established in 1259. The Friary was the general college for Augustinian friars in Ireland.

Turn left into Cecilia Street and left again into Temple Lane South and rejoin Dame Street. The three streets you have just walked along are typical medieval streets lined with largely seventeenth and eighteenth-century buildings. They are explored in more detail in *Around Temple Bar*. Back on **Dame Street**, turn right. Dame Street's name derives from the medieval church of St Mary del Dam, which was sited near City Hall. In medieval times, it was no more than a narrow track which connected the walled city to the area west of All Hallows Priory. Later, in the eighteenth century, it became an important thoroughfare, connecting the hierarchy in Dublin Castle with the Old Parliament and Trinity College.

At the Olympia Theatre, the street dips into a hollow. In Viking and medieval times, the River Poddle (more about this later) flowed along here – it now passes under the road. Cross Dame Street at the pedestrian lights opposite the Olympia. Directly ahead is the

Lower Castle Yard entrance into Dublin Castle. Continue up Dame Street for fifty metres to the traffic lights at Parliament Street. This is the site of **Dame Gate**, one of the principal gateways, long since demolished, which led into the walled city. Turn left immediately after City Hall [42] and enter **Dublin Castle** through the original stone gate. Above the gate is a statue of Justice facing into Upper Castle Yard. In harsher times it was frequently remarked upon that Justice had turned her back on its citizens. Further evidence of this was in the way the scales of justice hung unevenly – a result of the greater accumulation of rainwater in one of the scales. The authorities solved the problem by boring holes in both scales!

Dublin Castle was the seat of power for the ruling English establishment between 1220, when its construction was completed, and 1921, when the Treaty of Independence made it redundant. In 1317 the Castle was threatened by Edward de Bruce, and in 1534 it was beseiged, wholly unsuccessfully, by Silken Thomas Fitzgerald. Two famous escapes were made from the Castle, in 1591 and again in the following year, and both by the same man. Red Hugh O'Donnell, son of a Donegal chieftain, caused a minor sensation at the time by succeeding in lowering himself from a window in the Record Tower (in the Lower Castle Yard, beside the Chapel) and escaping – twice! Robert Emmet made a gallant but vain attempt at capturing the Castle in 1803 and,

**67**

Pearse Street Garda Station with Steyne Monument in foreground

on Easter Monday 1916, Irish Volunteers and members of the Irish Citizen Army gained entry to the Castle grounds and held out for a day on the roof of City Hall before being captured.

The original castle was an imposing structure, ranking in form and construction with the great castles of Europe at the time. It was a roughly rectangular enclosure with four very substantial cylindrical towers at the corners, a twin-towered gateway in the centre of one long wall and a small turret near the centre of the opposite long wall. Most of the original structure has long since disappeared, though the Upper Yard you are standing in is roughly the area of the original castle. Directly across the courtyard is the entrance to the eighteenth-century State Apartments.

Exit the Upper Castle Yard to the left and walk down into Lower Castle Yard. On your right is the ornate **Chapel Royal [45]** and **Record Tower**, both well worth a visit. Walk around the church and along the back of the Castle. On your left is a finely landscaped

garden with the restored Coach House in the background. The **River Poddle** formed a large and relatively deep pond at this point – it was known as **Dubh Linn** (Black Pool) – and it is the certain origin of the name Dublin. The river formed a natural moate around the south, east and north of the Castle and converged with the Liffey at a point nearby. The Vikings moored many of their longships at Dubh Linn. The superb Chester Beatty Library and Gallery of Oriental Art has recently moved here.

Continue, passing the Birmingham Tower on the right and leaving the Castle complex at **Ship Street Gate** directly ahead. Immediately to your right are the Castle Steps, built in the early nineteenth century. Beside the entrance to the steps, a wall plaque informs you that Jonathan Swift was born a hundred metres from here, in **Hoey's Court** (demolished). Running along Ship Street Little is a section of the old city wall. Turn left outside Ship Street Gate and walk up Ship Street Great. A wall plaque seventy metres up on the right tells you that this was the site of the church of **St Michael le Pole**, a Gaelic foundation whose accompanying round tower was ninety feet high.

Turn right at the top of Ship Street Great and walk 200 m to the traffic lights and admire the fine view, across St Patrick's Park, of St Patrick's Cathedral. Directly ahead, running down the right side of Bull Alley Street, with their copper-green domes, are Iveagh Buildings, built at the beginning of the century. Cross to the park and walk along the eastern end, away from Iveagh Buildings, keeping the railings on your right. Enter the park through the gate at the end of the railings.

**St Patrick's Park** was created by the then Guinness proprietor, Lord Iveagh, in 1901. Tenements between Bull Alley Street and St Patrick's Close at the other side of the cathedral were cleared to make way for the park and Iveagh Buildings in what was a major redevelopment and a vast improvement to the area. The park is an attractive space, with colourful flowerbeds, dense bushes and weather-worn trees. The **Liberty Bell** sculpture, by Adrienne Roche in 1988, on the right of the main avenue, is based on the early Christian St Patrick's Bell, on display in the National Museum. Walk to the end of the main avenue. A stone marker to the right of the gate tells you that this is the site of **St Patrick's Well**, where Ireland's patron saint is said to have baptised many people living in and around the locality. This was around the middle of the fifth century. A small church was founded by Patrick where today stands the magnificent **St Patrick's Cathedral**.

Turn and look at the cathedral, founded in 1191. It acquired cathedral status in 1213, and the Minot Tower was added in 1362. The building endured a turbulent history and, by 1864, was in danger of becoming a ruin. The predecessor of Lord Iveagh, Sir Benjamin Lee Guinness, came to the rescue, donating £160,000 towards its restoration and overseeing the four-year work by the architect Sir Thomas Drew. For a time, the cathedral was irreverently referred to as the Brewer's Church, after Sir Benjamin himself. Between 1901 and 1904, Lord Iveagh undertook a full restoration of the choir.

Exit the park at the gate beside St Patrick's Well, turn left and left again into St Patrick's Close, where you will find the main entrance to the cathedral. Beside the entrance is a seated statue of **Sir Benjamin**.

**Jonathan Swift [100]** was Dean of St Patrick's from 1713 until his death in 1745. He is buried near where you enter the cathedral, and lies beside his lifelong companion, Hester Johnson (Stella). The interior overflows with religious, familial and military monuments and it can be something of an overkill (excuse the militaristic pun) for some visitors. Among the most important memorials are mementoes to Swift, some Celtic gravestones, medieval brasses and tiles, memorials to the blind harpist and composer Carolan, the composer Michael William Balfe, and the first President of Ireland, Douglas Hyde.

Turn left when you leave the cathedral and continue past the graveyard to **Marsh's Library**, the oldest public library in Ireland, founded in 1701 by Archbishop Narcissus Marsh and opened in 1707. The building was designed by Sir William Robinson who had earlier designed the Royal Hospital Kilmainham. The original brick façade was replaced in the

**69**

nineteenth century with a mixture of stone and brick. An interesting feature of the library, unchanged since the eighteenth century, are the three wired alcoves within which readers consulted rare books that were chained to the walls. The Library contains about 25,000 books, some dating from the sixteenth century, together with 250 volumes of manuscripts and many maps.

Continue to the end of St Patrick's Close and go left for ten metres to look at the stone entrance pillars to the long-since demolished **St Sepulchre's Archepiscopal Palace**. The palace was built by the Anglo-Norman Archbishop Comyn, who also built St Patrick's Cathedral. The site is now occupied by Kevin Street Garda Station.

Retrace your steps and continue along Upper Kevin Street and past the Dean's residence. Fifty metres past the deanery is number 35/35A, the only surviving 'Dutch Billy' house in the area, identifiable by its gable end facing the street. These houses, very common in Dublin in the sixteenth and seventeenth century, were named after King William (Billy) of Orange and were occupied mainly by the French Protestant Huguenots living in the Liberties. The **'Liberties'** was an extensive area south and west of the walled city, defined by the fact that it was outside the civil jurisdiction of the mayor and council of the medieval city.

At the traffic lights, turn right and walk past the cathedral and the park. English plane and lime trees line this western side of the park. In what is now the Liberties Vocational School mid-way up Bull Alley Street on your right (no need to go up) was the 'Bayno', a play centre built in 1915 for the children from around the area. The name is derived from 'beano', or feast.

Continue along Patrick Street and turn right after the shops into Bride Road. The Iveagh Fitness & Leisure Centre is on your left, once the home of the Victorian **Iveagh Baths** and now a listed building (for heritage reasons). Opposite the old Baths is the Iveagh Hostel, for homeless men. At the end of Bride Road is Bride Street. Both are named after the church of St Bride, demolished during the development of the Iveagh Trust Buildings at the beginning of the 1900s. The church was an important place of worship in medieval times until the parish was united with the parish of St Werburgh's in 1886. This entire area was radically altered during the Iveagh development, with medieval streets and laneways disappearing without trace.

Turn left and go up as far as St Werburgh's Church, 150 m along on the right. Thirty metres before the church is a passage leading to a Department of Social Welfare local office. The building occupies the approximate site of **Hoey's Court**, where Jonathan Swift was born in 1667.

The present **St Werburgh's Church** dates from 1759 and has one of the finest eighteenth-century church interiors in Dublin. It also had a magnificent fifty-metre high tower and spire, but this was removed in the early nineteenth century following the rebellion of 1803, the authorities fearing that it could be used in a future attack on the Castle. A fire in 1754 destroyed much of the interior of Thomas Burgh's original 1715 building. The body of Lord Edward Fitzgerald, who was killed during the rebellion of 1798, is interred in the church's vault.

At the top of Werburgh Street, turn left into **Christchurch Place**, formerly Skinners Row, so named on account of the numerous traders in hides and skins who lived on the five-metre wide street. The street was radically altered in the early nineteenth century and was renamed Christchurch Place.

Walk past Jury's Hotel to the traffic lights. Where the Peace Garden is located is the approximate site of the **Tholsel**, erected at the beginning of the fourteenth century. The Tholsel was the City Hall, and the Lord Mayor of the city was chosen here on Michaelmas day. The building deteriorated towards the end of the eighteenth century – courts which used to take place there were moved to Green Street Courthouse, north of the Liffey, and the meetings of Dublin Corporation were transferred to the City Assembly House in South William Street. In 1809, the Tholsel was demolished. Across the street from where the Tholsel was sited was the city's **High Cross**, another medieval focal point, but which disappeared long before the Tholsel. It was the custom of the day to read proclamations and make other

Christ Church

public pronouncements to the city's citizenry at this cross.

If you wish to visit **Christ Church Cathedral**, this is the best point on the tour to do it. Press the button and wait patiently for the green man. Once you have crossed, go right until you reach the entrance gates to the cathedral grounds.

The Viking King, Sigtryggr Silkbeard had a small wooden church built in 1038, where Christ Church stands, for the first bishop of Dublin, Dunan. The Norman Earl of Pembroke, Richard de Clare (Strongbow) rebuilt the church in stone for the archbishop of Dublin, Laurence O'Toole whose status was later raised to Saint Laurence, patron saint of Dublin. The church, which was begun in 1172, was still under construction in 1176 when Strongbow died, and also in 1180 when Laurence O'Toole died. A memorial to Strongbow can be seen in the present day cathedral's nave, while the heart of St Laurence is in a thirteenth-century reliquary in the chapel of St Laud, one of the cathedral's small interior chapels.

The crypt is the oldest intact building in Dublin, dating to the original construction in 1172. Over the centuries the cathedral suffered many ignominies, not least the use being made of the vaults as taverns and the nave as a market in the late 1500s. In 1562 the nave vaulting collapsed bringing with it the south wall. The replacement was structurally unsound and the cathedral was in such a state of disrepair by the mid 1800s that there was a real threat to its survival. Not to be outdone by Sir Benjamin Lee Guinness' magnanimous gesture in providing the money for the restoration of nearby St Patrick's cathedral in 1864 (Guinness at the time was Dublin's largest employer and Sir

Christ Church doorway

Benjamin was carrying on a Guinness tradition of providing money for public projects in Dublin), Henry Roe, a Dublin whiskey distiller, coughed up a whopping £250,000 and saved this great cathedral from certain ruin. The English architect George Edmund Street was commissioned to restore the building and the restoration took place between 1871 and 1878. Street's finished product was highly controversial, embellishing the main structure with elaborate flying buttresses and adding an annexe to the immediate west of the cathedral.

All that remains above ground of the original cathedral are the north wall, the transepts and the western part of the choir. In the grounds of the cathedral are the chapter house remains of the Augustinian Priory, abandoned at the time of the Reformation. Almost certainly, the remains of other buildings belonging to the priory lie under Christchurch Place.

When you leave the cathedral, retrace your footsteps to the Peace Garden at the other side of Christchurch Place. With your back to the cathedral, cross to the right to the opposite side of Nicholas Street (continuation of Patrick Street) and go left before the Woodchester building and immediately right into **Back Lane**. **Tailor's Hall**, halfway along the lane on the right, behind the old stone gateway, is the oldest guild hall in Ireland. Built in 1706, it housed, naturally enough, the Tailor's Guild which, along with other trade guilds, exercised considerable influence on the city's commerce. In December 1792, political gatherings which were to become known as the 'Back Lane Parliament', took place in this building over a six-day period in a bid to put pressure on the English throne to grant concessions to Catholics. (At the time, Catholics in Ireland were excluded from the army, parliament, law, government service and other areas of public life.) Today, the Tailor's Hall is the headquarters of the Irish National Trust (An Taisce).

Continue to the end of Back Lane and turn left into Cornmarket, which leads on to Thomas Street. After fifty metres, stop to have a look at the section of the original city wall, standing as a lonely reminder that a medieval city did once exist here. This is also where the **Cornmarket** of medieval Dublin was situated. Directly across the street is the site of **Newgate**, once the principal western city gate, long since demolished. Immediately west of Newgate was a six-metre deep and twelve-metre wide defence ditch, providing some comfort to the oft-besieged citizens of the walled city. The three other sides of the city were surrounded by water.

Continue for fifty metres to where Francis Street goes off to the left. Cross to the right side of Thomas Street here. Down the hill runs St Augustine Street, in the direction of the River Liffey. This seemingly insignificant corner of Thomas Street and St Augustine Street was once a major crossroads where the ancient roads of pre-Viking Ireland crossed: the Slige

Mór to the west, the Slige Midluachra to the north, and the Slige Chualann to the south.

Continue along Thomas Street for a hundred metres to the **Church of St Augustine and St John the Baptist**, popularly known as John's Lane Church and designed by Edward Welby Pugin and George Ashlin. It was built between 1862 and 1895 and its dramatic, 231-foot high, granite and red sandstone spire can be seen for many miles. Inside, the 152-foot long nave, the high ceiling and the fine stained glass windows combine with the magnificent exterior to make this one of Dublin's finest churches – it is no wonder, then, that John Ruskin described it as a 'poem in stone'. The building has benefited enormously from a recent restoration costing over one million pounds.

Turn right beyond the church into the cobbled John's Lane West, formerly the site of **St John's Hospital**, originally founded in the twelfth century. The hospital was run by Augustinians but was suppressed in 1539. Its eighty-foot high round tower was demolished around 1800.

Continue down and around John's Lane and, at the very end, when you cannot continue any further, turn left into St Augustine Street. Turn right after twenty metres into Wormwood Gate, named after one of the medieval city gates. This will bring you to the middle of Lower Bridge Street. Before crossing to Cook Street, directly ahead, go left for fifty metres and have a look at the **Brazen Head**, Dublin's oldest pub

Dublin [147]. Thirsty work, this walking!
Castle      Cross and walk along **Cook Street**, lined on the right by a high stone wall. Some of the stones were brought across the Liffey from the demolished 1224 Dominican foundation, the Abbey of St Saviour. Other parts are from the original city wall. After 150 m, go through **St Audoen's Gate** (1240), the only surviving gate to the old walled city. Climb the old steps to the park above. Near the top of the steps, on your left, is the original entrance to the Anglican **Church of St Audoen**, a church built on the site of the sixth-century church of St Columcille. The doorway is the oldest remaining part of the church, dating from about 1200. The tower is seventeenth century. Before climbing the last few steps to High Street, have a brief look around the park on the right.

Turn left on High Street and walk past, first, the Anglican St Audoen's and next, the Catholic **St Audoen's**, designed by Patrick Byrne and built in 1837. Both churches take their name from St Ouen of Rouen, in Normandy, France. Turn left at the traffic

lights and walk down **Winetavern Street**, so named on account of the wine merchants who traded here. The street runs underneath the stone arch which connects the cathedral to the Synod Hall. On your left is the entrance to **Dublinia**, a Viking Interpretative Centre, with Viking streets, smells and Viking 'inhabitants' – all recreated to give the visitor a visual sense of Viking Dublin.

Halfway down the hill was where King's Gate, another of the old city gates, was located. On the steep incline down to the Liffey, you pass the gigantic 'Bunkers' of Dublin Corporation on the right. This was undoubtedly the most controversial site to be developed in Dublin in modern times. During the process of digging the very deep foundations, a vast landscape of early Viking remains were uncovered. Despite vociferous street protests (20,000 protesters marched on the construction site on one memorable day in the late 1970s), the Corporation went ahead and built their precious bunkers, thus destroying what would have been a unique open-air Viking museum.

As you cross Cook Street on your journey down the hill, you can see perfectly the top half of the Onion Tower [79], half a mile away in the Guinness Brewery. Descend to the river. The earliest Custom House in Dublin, known as **The Crane**, was located at the bottom of Winetavern Street. The bridge upstream (left) of the one in front of you, O'Donovan Rossa Bridge, is **Father Mathew Bridge**, the site of Áth Cliath, or *the ford of the hurdles*. It consisted of mounds of stones at regular intervals over which were placed logs and branches to form the only bridge across the Liffey. Today, the Gaelic name for Dublin is Baile Átha Cliath, or *the town of the hurdleford*.

Across the Liffey are the **Four Courts**, site of the 1224 Dominican priory referred to when you were on Cook Street. Other medieval locations within easy walking distance on the north side of the river are the **Church of St Michan [88]** on Church Street, the old **Chapter House of St Mary's Abbey [95]** on Meetinghouse Lane, and **St Mary's Church [62]** on the corner of Mary Street and Jervis Street.

Turn right and walk along **Wood Quay** for 200 m, passing as you go the headquarters of Dublin Corporation. The original plan was for four 'bunkers' to be built, but such was the uproar over the first two – not to mention the cost – that the Corporation sat on the original plan, eventually deciding to go for the easy option and build this more conventional block on Wood Quay.

Turn right into **Fishamble Street**, one of the oldest streets in the city. Excavations indicate that the line of the street has remained unchanged since at least AD 950. In medieval times, Fishamble Street was the city market for fish which was openly displayed on the individual traders' stalls, or 'shambles', hence the origin of the street's name. The old house on the corner of Essex Street West and Fishamble Street, fifty metres up, is believed to be the oldest inhabited houses in Dublin. Essex

Street West was formerly called **Smock Alley**, after a famous theatre of the same name on the street. Twenty metres further up Fishamble Street and on the left, a wall plaque beside the entrance to the new George Frideric Handel Hotel relates that the old **Musick Hall**, designed by the Georgian architect Richard Castle in 1741, stood on this site and that the first ever public performance of *Messiah* took place here in 1742 **[30]**.

Go back down Fishamble Street and take the last turning on the right before Wood Quay. This is **Exchange Street**, known in medieval times as Blind Alley. The beautiful old **Church of St Michael and John**, fifty metres along on the right, has been transformed into a Viking interpretative centre.

As the street swings to the right, you can see on the left, behind and below the specially designed gates, the remains of **Isolde's Tower**, a forty-foot high round tower at the north-eastern corner of the old city walls. Continue. At the junction of Upper and Lower Exchange Streets and Essex Gate is the site of **Buttevants Tower**, demolished in 1675 to make **Essex Gate**, also demolished.

To finish the tour, go left onto Parliament Street, cross into Essex Street and stroll through **Temple Bar**. You will be walking through a medieval streetscape which, in every other sense, is utterly modern and commercial. Refreshment possibilities are too many to mention around here, so I will leave you to your own devices.

An interesting stroll through a part of Dublin which has changed relatively little over the years. The Guinness Brewery, of course, has moved with the times, but the shadow-laden, cobbled streets and the enormous nineteenth-century warehouses which line them are still here. Further west, the seventeenth-century Royal Hospital today houses the excellent Museum of Modern Art.

The tour can be completed in a morning or an afternoon, however you can easily make a leisurely day of it, beginning with a visit to the Guinness Hop Store followed by a light lunch in the Royal Hospital Kilmainham. In the afternoon, visit the Museum of Modern Art and perhaps Kilmainham Gaol, before completing the tour in time for an aperitif in a city centre pub.

**Tour begins:** *at the corner of Thomas Street and Meath Street, opposite The Clock pub.*

Walk west, away from the city, along the busy trading thoroughfare of Thomas Street, until you come to a church on the left. This is **St Catherine's Church**, at 112 acres once the second largest Dublin city parish. It was designed by John Smyth (he also designed the landmark Poolbeg lighthouse in Dublin Bay) and built between 1762 and 1769. A tower was added in the late eighteenth century and, in 1845, the church underwent a major restoration. In the opinion of a leading authority on Georgian Dublin, St Catherine's possesses the most elegant classical church façade in Dublin. The church is unusual in that the main entrance is located in the centre of the north wall, and not in the west end, as would normally have been the case. It was built on the site of a twelfth-century church whose original construction was to honour Thomas à Becket, archbishop of Canterbury, on the

## Tour Facts

- **Length of tour:** 4.4 miles (7 kilometres)
- **Duration of tour:** at a leisurely stroll, approximately 2½ hours
- **Refreshments:** during the tour (Guinness Hop Store; Heuston Station; Museum of Modern Art; Kilmainham Gaol); after the tour (the Brazen Head on Lower Bridge Street; Jury's Hotel or the Lord Edward pub on Christchurch Place)
- **Getting to the Starting Point:** from O'Connell Bridge (walk west [upriver] along the south [left] quays for half-a-mile, turn left at The Merchant pub and walk to the top of Lower Bridge Street. Turn right into Cornmarket and Thomas Street and walk for three hundred metres to the junction with Meath Street on your left); from Trinity front gates (walk the length of Dame Street and Lord Edward Street, go past Christ Church Cathedral and walk to the end of High Street. Continue on to Thomas Street and walk three hundred metres to the junction with Meath Street on your left)

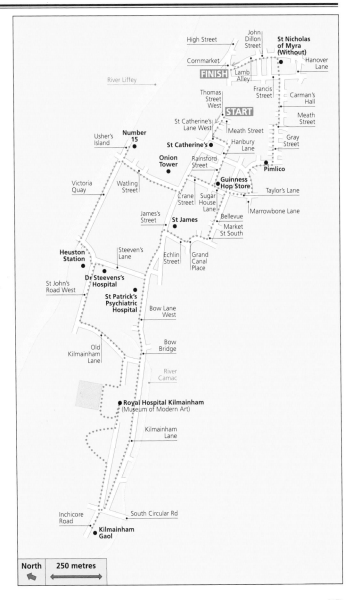

North

250 metres

## Opening Times

- **Guinness Hop Store**
  Telephone (01) 408 4800
  1 April–30 September:
  Mon–Sat 9.30am–last
  admission 5pm
  Sunday/Bank Holidays
  10.30am–last admission 4.30pm
  1 October–31March:
  Mon–Sat 9.30am–last
  admission 4pm
  Sunday/Bank Holidays
  12pm–last admission 4pm
- **Irish Museum of Modern Art (RHK)**
  Telephone (01) 612 9900
  Tues–Sat 10am–5.30pm
  Sunday/Bank Holidays
  12pm–5.30pm
  Closed Monday
- **Kilmainham Gaol**
  Telephone (01) 453 5984
  April–September
  Every day 9.30am–last
  admission 4.45pm
  October–March
  Mon–Fri 9.30am–last admission
  4pm
  Sunday 10am–last admission
  4.45pm
  Closed Saturday

orders of King Henry II. In 1803 the patriot Robert Emmet was executed across the street from the church. The building has recently been restored by the Church of Ireland organisation, CORE, as a place of worship for all Christian denominations.

Go left before the church, up the narrow St Catherine's Lane West. In the nineteenth century the neighbourhood was comprised of laneways and alleyways similar to this, at either side of which were tenements built so closely together that adequate hygiene and sanitation was impossible. Turn right into Hansbury Lane, passing on your right a small park and graveyard at the back of the church. Continue in a straight line into Rainsfort Street.

You are surrounded by Guinness warehouses and vathouses. Directly ahead is a huge wooden doorway, emblazoned with the words *Guinness – St James Street Brewery*. The narrow gauge rail tracks running along the middle of the road are a remnant of the extensive transport system the brewery developed over time.

At the end of Rainsfort Street, turn left into Sugar House Lane. The entrance to the **Guinness Hop Store** is on your immediate left, in a converted nineteenth-century warehouse. Inside, visitors can watch an audiovisual show on the history of the brewery and can visit the museum.

Arthur Guinness was thirty-four when he acquired Rainsford Brewery in 1759, establishing a 9,000-year lease (obviously, he believed in reincarnation) at a rent of £45 a year at St James's Gate. His entrepreneurial skill and boundless energy transformed, within his own lifetime, a moderately-sized brewery and one of fifty-five in Dublin into the city's largest.

Arthur died in 1803 and his sons Arthur, Benjamin and William Luttrell took over the running of the business. Arthur outlived his two brothers and assumed sole ownership and, when he died in 1855, his son Benjamin inherited the entire concern. He would later become Sir Benjamin Lee Guinness and is remembered today as the restorer of St Patrick's Cathedral. When he died in 1868, he left the brewery to his sons Arthur and Edward Cecil, later to become Lords Ardilaun and Iveagh. Lord Iveagh is remembered for the extensive social housing developments near St Patrick's Cathedral and for the establishment of St Patrick's Park, while his brother Lord Ardilaun is remembered for the formal laying out of St Stephen's Green and for rebuilding the Coombe Lying-In Hospital.

In its earliest days, the brewery did not produce stout (it was then known as porter, originating from the porters in London's Covent Garden whose favoured drink it was). When Arthur decided to try his luck at brewing porter, it was to prove a decisive commercial move. Production began in earnest and Guinness's never looked back from that moment.

By the time the brewery was publicly floated and became a limited liability company – in 1886 – it employed over 2,600 people and was easily the largest brewery in the world. The Guinness complex today occupies about sixty acres, has offices across the globe and produces over ten million glasses of the creamy-topped porter *every day*.

There was no shortage of consumers of alcohol back in the early days. Records show that there were an estimated 1,180 ale-houses and ninety-two brew-houses in Dublin in the seventeenth century. It was common for wealthy families to have their own brewing plant and the housewives in these families were often quite expert brewers. There was, of course, a downside to all of this and it is no surprise to learn that the consumption of alcohol was considered to be one of the greatest social evils of the period. In the eighteenth century the practice of household brewing declined and the job of brewing was gradually taken in hand by public brewers such as Guinness's.

Turn right when you leave the Hop Store and walk in a straight line – if you can – along Crane Street (formerly Crane Lane) to the end. Turn left into James Street. The residence of the first Arthur Guinness is immediately on your left. Beside the house is St James's Gate, a stone archway leading into the brewery. The original St James's Gate stood near this spot, but at right angles, and was the western gate which separated the inner and outer suburbs of medieval Dublin.

Cross James Street at this point and walk down Watling Street opposite. A wall plaque on the corner building opposite the bank quotes from James Joyce's *Ulysses*:

*'Mr Kernan turned and walked down the slope of Watling Street by the corner of Guinness's Visitors waiting room.'*

The Rupert Guinness Theatre is on your left as you descend the hill. The Abbey players performed here for two months following the fire which destroyed the Abbey Theatre in 1951. To your right is a fine view of the Onion Tower, built as a windmill by the previous tenant of this site, Henry Roe. Roe

A pint of plain please!

was a whiskey distiller and is remembered to this day as the benefactor whose extraordinary generosity saved Christ Church Cathedral from becoming a ruin. The tower is 150 feet high and 70 feet in diameter at the base and is believed to be the biggest windmill tower ever built in the British Isles. St Patrick acts as a weathervane on the top.

At the traffic lights at the bottom of the hill once stood the Watling Street Gatehouse. The gateway, built in 1812, was removed stone by stone in 1847, soon after the opening of Kingsbridge (now Heuston) Station, as the additional vehicular traffic coming from and going to the station was causing terrible congestion at the Gatehouse. It was re-assembled at the entrance to the Royal Hospital in Kilmainham. (I can't decide whether it's reassuring or depressing to learn that Dublin has had traffic jams for over 150 years. Long live walking tours!)

Before you turn left onto Victoria Quay, walk right along Usher's Island for about a hundred metres until you come to a quayside house which adjoins the new apartments (as I write, it is painted a dark brown and is seriously run-down and in danger of demolition). The house is number 15 Usher's Island and was the home of James Joyce's great-aunts, Mrs Lyons and Mrs Callanan and her daugher Mary Ellen. In 1987, the American film director John Huston made a full-length feature film of Joyce's short-story, *The Dead*. Huston was too ill to travel to Ireland, but he insisted that all the exterior scenes in the story be shot on location in Dublin. This house is prominently featured in the story – Joyce's best known – and in Huston's film.

*'He continued scraping his feet vigorously while the three women went upstairs, laughing, to the ladies' dressing-room. A light fringe of snow lay like a cape on the shoulders of his overcoat and like toecaps on the toes of his galoshes; and, as the buttons of his overcoat slipped with a squeaking noise through the snow-stiffened frieze, a cold, fragrant air from out-of-doors escaped from crevices and folds.'* From *The Dead*.

Retrace your steps. On the corner of Watling Street and Usher's Island is a Simon Community Night Shelter, providing accommodation for Dublin's growing numbers of homeless people. Proceed along Victoria Quay towards Heuston Station. You will get a better overall view if you cross to the river side, but be very careful in doing so – the speeding cars and trucks take no prisoners along here. The massive obelisk which is the Wellington Monument can be easily seen ahead, poking its upper half above the Phoenix Park trees. On your left, the high wall obliterates your view of the brewery. Across the river beyond the open field is the National Museum, recently converted from Collins Army Barracks. Continue along the quayside to the large Guinness gates on the left. The brewery had its very own jetty on the river at this point, from which ten purpose-built Guinness barges began their long journey along the intricate inland waterway system to their destinations north, west and south.

At the end of the quay is Heuston Bridge (1827-8), named after Seán Heuston, one of the 1916 Easter Rising rebels. Cross over to Heuston Station, formerly Kingsbridge. It bears the date 1844, however a stonemasons' strike delayed its completion until 1848. It is easily Dublin's most impressive railway station and is in fact regarded by many railway enthusiasts as one of the finest stations in Europe.

Go left around the front of the station and cross the dual-carriageway at the pedestrian lights to the impressive and imposing Dr Steevens's Hospital, founded in 1720 and opened thirteen years later. Jonathan Swift was on the hospital board during its earliest years. The building is now in the hands of the Eastern Health Board. A recent restoration managed to introduce to the city a building which we had all either forgotten about or had never really noticed. Although it was built at the end of the nineteenth century, its style resembles a Queen Anne building (very early eighteenth-century) and bears no relation to Victorian architecture. Walk along the left side of the building, up Steeven's Lane, to view the fine Georgian front of the hospital and to make a closer examination (!) of the graceful Thomas Burgh design (Burgh also designed the Old Library in Trinity College).

Go back down Steeven's Lane and turn left and walk for about two hundred metres, keeping the station on your right. Go left into Old Kilmainham Lane (not marked) where the signpost points to **Museum of Modern Art, Royal Hospital Kilmainham**. Trees overhang this quiet road and there is something of a rural and ancient feel to the area. Two stone pillars ahead mark the entrance to the *RHK, Museum of Modern Art*. Walk up the tree-lined avenue.

*[If you happen to be doing the tour and the RHK is closed, you can continue the tour by proceeding along the road you are on and turning left into Bow Lane West at the bottom of the hill. Turn to page 83 and continue the tour.]*

The architectural style of the Royal Hospital Kilmainham is based on Les Invalides in Paris. With a formal façade, spacious courtyard and fine interior, it is arguably Ireland's finest seventeenth-century monumental building. It was designed by Sir William Robinson and completed in 1685 and served as a home for retired soldiers for almost 250 years, at the same time that the Chelsea Hospital in London was offering similar services. The Royal Hospital clients were frequently referred to as Chelsea pensioners.

In 1986 the Irish Government restored the long-neglected building at a cost of £21 million and, in 1991, it re-opened its doors as the Irish Museum of Modern Art (IMMA). The Museum houses a permanent collection of Irish and international art of the twentieth century, as well as visiting exhibitions throughout the year. In addition, the annual programme features live music and theatrical performances.

Go right at the top of the driveway and walk around to the front (northern) side. Stretching away and down the hill to your right are formal gardens, undergoing major redevelopment and well on the way to becoming, once again, an important feature of the entire complex. Walk down to the terrace above the gardens and look back at the magnificent hospital façade, with the enormous elongated windows, fine clock tower and copper-pointed dome.

Continue your journey around the building and enter the graceful, gravel-layered courtyard through the West Arch. To visit the Museum of Modern Art, walk right and across the courtyard and enter the building through the glass doors.

Exit the courtyard through the West Arch and walk away from the main building. After twenty metres, a narrow, tarmacadamed pathway leads off to the right. Take this path and descend into

what can only be described as a wild meadow. It's a pleasant feeling to be able to walk through here and know that you are only a short walk from the hustle and bustle of the city centre. At the bottom of the hill, go left along the same pathway and swing left up the steep hill towards the main avenue. From this vantage point it is worth turning around to look again at the Royal Hospital, now partly hidden by a line of trees.

Rejoin the main avenue and turn right, stopping after twenty metres at the closed gate which is the entrance to two old cemeteries. **Bully's Acre** is one of Dublin's oldest cemeteries. It contains a large, tenth-century decorated granite cross shaft, possibly the remains of a boundary cross of St Maigneann's monastery, founded in 606. Tradition has it that Brian Boru camped here before the Battle of Clontarf in 1014 and that, following the battle, the bodies of his slain son Murrough and grandson Turlough were interred near the cross. Dan Donnelly, the famous Irish boxer is also buried here (minus his arm, which is in a glass case in a pub in Kilcullen, Co. Kildare – *out of 'arm's way*, one could say). Robert Emmet was buried here in 1803, before he was taken to an unknown location where he was finally laid to rest. Otherwise, the cemetery contains the remains of monks, knights, princes and Dublin citizens. The other cemetery contains the graves of Chelsea pensioners, as well as the graves of some British troops killed in the 1916 Easter Rising.

Continue to the Richmond Tower, the gateway at the end of

the avenue. It formerly stood at the junction of Watling Street and Victoria Quay (you passed by there early on in the tour) and was called the Watling Street Gatehouse. Built of Dublin calp limestone, it was designed by Francis Johnston and opened by the Lord Lieutenant the Duke of Richmond.

Cross to Inchicore Road, opposite the Tower. Kilmainham Courthouse is on your left and, beside it, **Kilmainham Gaol**, a building steeped in Ireland's turbulent history. Political prisoners over the years included Robert Emmet, Charles Stewart Parnell, Isaac Butt, William Smith O'Brien and Constance Markievicz. There were many others. For example, Anne Devlin, a loyal supporter and close friend of Emmet who, despite enduring brutally inhumane treatment during her three-year incarceration – mostly in solitary confinement – refused stoically to give any information to her captors. For many, however, it is the fact that the leaders of the 1916 Easter Rising were executed here which gives Kilmainham Gaol its particular status. The building is now a museum and is open to the public.

Retrace your steps and cross to the Richmond Tower, turning right and immediately left into Kilmainham Lane. This road was once known as Moldering Lane (from Murdering Lane) and was a popular route along which robbers would wait in hiding for unsuspecting travellers to pass by, whereupon the unfortunate victim would be set upon, robbed and occasionally murdered into the bargain.

Stop for a moment opposite Kilmainham Garda Station and look across the valley to the Little Sisters of the Poor Convent, on the brow of the hill. The building was recently converted into luxury appartments. Below you is Rowerstown Lane and other quiet little roads making up the close-knit community in the sleepy hollow, through which flows the River Camac. Continue along Kilmainham Lane. As you proceed, the road begins to curve and descend between terraced houses and overgrown wild flowers, giving to the vicinity a beguilingly rural atmosphere. Pass on your right Willie Birmingham Place, a modest housing development built by Alone, a charitable organisation for single or widowed elderly citizens. Take the time to read the witty, 'self-described life of Willie Bermingham', reproduced on a limestone plaque at the entrance to the estate.

At the bottom of the hill the road becomes for a brief spell Camac Terrace. The road left leads to the entrance to the RHK which you passed through some time ago. *[This is the point where you will rejoin the tour if the grounds of the RHK were closed.]* As you cross the River Camac – which enters the Liffey beside Heuston Station – have a look at the ascending steps leading to the upper road on your right. These are known as Cromwell's Quarters and refer to Henry Cromwell, the fourth son of the infamous Oliver. Henry was the governor-general of

Onion Tower

Ireland from 1655 to 1659.

Continue into Bow Lane West and up the long, straight hill. Midway along and on the left, look through the large iron gates into the grounds and main building of **St Patrick's Psychiatric Hospital**, founded in 1745, the year that Jonathan Swift died. Swift had left a legacy worth in the region of £11,000 towards the hospital's foundation, a bequest prompted by his belief that his illness was a psychiatric one, though it is now known that this was not the case. He wrote some typically satiric lines relating to the bequest:

*'He gave the little wealth he had,*

*To build a house for fools and mad;*

*And show'd by one satyric touch,*

*No nation wanted it so much.'*

Continue and, at the top of the hill, cross Steeven's Lane and proceed in the same direction along James Street. On your immediate right is a pedestrian island with a thirty-foot high obelisk and fountain. Up to relatively recent times funerals which passed here went around this island three times before moving on to the cemetery.

Continue to the pedestrian lights beside the Guinness Medical Department and opposite St James Parochial Hall. Cross at the lights and go up Echlin Street, passing along the side of the Parochial Hall and St James Catholic Church. The rounded building at the top of the street was originally the Canal Maltings building and adjoined the Guinness Canal Basin. The building is virtually unchanged, but houses a furniture business today. An extension to the Grand Canal brought the inland waterway into the Guinness complex here in order that the porter could be transported by horse-drawn barge to Limerick and Ballinasloe in County Galway, and eastwards to Ringsend where it was exported by ship. The brewery extended down to the Liffey and, in 1872, was operating ten barges to and from a purpose-built jetty down river from Heuston Bridge (passed earlier on the tour).

The original line of the canal from Suir Road Bridge to St James' Harbour was filled in in the early 1970s. The Bird Cage bridge, the two harbours with their metal bridge, the dry docks and, more recently, the Harbour Master's house, have all disappeared.

Turn left at the end of Echlin Street and walk along the bend in the road and take a left into Market Street. Walk between the impressive warehouses on your left and right, feeling dwarfed and a little like Gulliver in *Brobdingnag*. When you reach the Hop Store car park, turn right into Taylor's Lane and cut through the pedestrian passageway to Marrowbone Lane. Cross at the pedestrian lights directly ahead and turn left and walk along Marrowbone Lane. Dublin Corporation flats are on your left and right along here.

After about a hundred metres, turn right into Pimlico and walk until you come to the Pimlico Tavern, a couple of hundred metres along. Cross and enter Grey Street, directly across the street from the pub. Ahead is a statue of the Sacred Heart, erected by the parishioners of St Catherine's 'to the honour and glory of God and in commemoration of the centenary of the Emancipation 1929'. It was restored to mark the visit of Pope John Paul II to the Liberties [**70**] on 29 September 1979.

There are four small, urban squares off Grey Street, all single-storey terraced cottages – Brabazon, Meath, Gray and Reginald – and all worth exploring. Walk to the end of Grey Street and stand on the pavement of the busy Meath Street. Explore the street a little if you like before going right and immediately left into Carman's Hall. Directly ahead is the Catholic Church of **St Nicholas of Myra (Without)** (1829) on Francis Street. Walk to the church. The 'Without' derives from the fact that it was one of

two older churches in the locality, one 'within' the walled city, the other 'without'. The church is near the site of an important Franciscan Friary which lay outside the city walls during medieval times. Francis Street is named after this Friary.

Explore Francis Street in your own time; it is noted for its antique furniture shops. If the church gates are open, go through and, keeping the church on your right, walk through into John Dillon Street, lined with terraced two-storey, red-brick houses. Turn left into John Dillon Street. If access to John Dillon Street is closed off via the church grounds, turn right into Francis Street and left into Hanover Lane and left again into John Dillon Street.

Proceed along John Dillon Street until you see in front of you the back entrance to the Iveagh Markets. Go along Lamb Alley, keeping the walls of the Market on your left. At the end of Lamb Alley, examine the section of old wall on the right. This is a section of the original wall which surrounded the old city.

At this junction – of Cornmarket and Lamb Alley – you can see across the main street to your right St Audoen's Protestant and Catholic churches, and across the Liffey, the copper-green dome of the Four Courts.

*Your tour ends here. Dublin's oldest pub, the Brazen Head [147], is down Lower Bridge Street opposite, and may be an interesting place to wet your lips. Alternatively, walk right along High Street towards the city centre.*

A tour which takes you off the beaten path, away from the 'star attractions', along unfashionable streets which form part of the old, rapidly changing, city.

Walk part of the route of one of Europe's most ancient highways, stand on the vast public space which was once Dublin's cattle market, and visit the place of interment of the 1916 Easter Rising leaders. Elsewhere, discover St Michan's Church, with its fascinating vaults and its associations with George Frideric Handel; the Old Jameson Distillery; the National Museum in Collins Barracks; the impressive eighteenth-century former Bluecoat School; and the twelfth-century Chapter-House of St Mary's Abbey.

Complete the tour in a morning or an afternoon, or make a day of it, stopping for lunch along the way.

## Tour Facts

- **Length of tour:** 4 miles (6.4 kilometres)
- **Duration of tour:** a leisurely 2 hours
- **Refreshments:** during the tour (the Museum Café; Ryan's pub on Parkgate Street); after the tour (Slattery's on Capel Street; Keating's on the corner of Abbey and Jervis Streets; local coffee shops)
- **Getting to the Starting Point:** from O'Connell Bridge, walk away from the sea along the south (left) quays until you get to the beginning of Merchant's Quay, just beyond the Civic Offices on Wood Quay and directly opposite the Four Courts

 **Tour begins:** *on Merchant's Quay, looking over at the Four Courts.*

Spend a few minutes admiring the Four Courts [**63**], designed by James Gandon, and considered by some to be the city's finest eighteenth-century public building.

Go right and cross O'Donovan Rossa Bridge and stand at the corner of the Four Courts and Chancery Place. Turn around and look across the river and up the hill at Christ Church Cathedral [**71**], the crypt of which is Dublin's oldest standing structure (1172). Below it, on Wood Quay, are the modern Civic Offices [**30**] of Dublin Corporation.

Walk away from the river, along Chancery Place. Directly ahead is River House, a dismal, concrete office block which is home to the Motor Tax and Licence section of Dublin Corporation. The building is on the site of Donnelly's Pub, where the boxer Dan Donnelly died in 1820. Donnelly was perhaps Ireland's greatest boxer. His punch was so fierce that his boxing arm was preserved and is on display in a pub (not *The Donnelly Arms*) in Kilcullen, Co. Kildare. Beside River House is Hughes Pub, where you can, on occasion, be lucky to stumble upon a terrific, impromptu

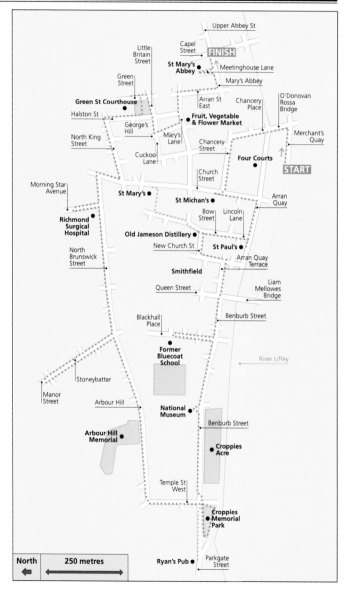

## Opening Times

- **St Michan's Church and Vaults**
  Telephone (01) 872 4154
  Mon–Fri 10am–12.45pm;
  2pm–4.45pm
  Saturday 10am–12.45pm
  Sunday Services 10am
- **The Old Jameson Distillery**
  Telephone (01) 807 2355
  Open every day
  9.30am–last tour 5pm
- **National Museum at Collins Barracks**
  Telephone (01) 677 7444
  Tues–Sat 10am–5pm
  Sunday 2pm–5pm
  Closed Monday
- **Arbour Hill 1916 Memorial**
  Normally open every day
  10am–dusk (times not guaranteed)
- **Dublin Corporation Fruit, Vegetable and Flower Market**
  Mon–Fri 6am–3pm
  Saturday 7.30am–11am
  Closed Sunday
- **St Mary's Abbey Chapter House**
  Telephone (01) 872 1490
  Mid-June–Mid-September
  Sunday and Wednesday
  10am–5pm
  (phone for confirmation of opening times)

traditional music session. It's a low-key (!) venue, away from the hustle and bustle of Temple Bar.

Turn left and walk along Chancery Street. The Dublin Metropolitan District Courthouse is on your right and, beside it, the Bridewell Garda Station, built between 1901 and 1906. When you reach Church Street, cross diagonally right to view **St**

**Michan's Protestant Church**. The church's foundation dates to 1095 when Michan, a Danish bishop, built a church on this site. Until 1697, it was the only parish church north of the Liffey and is, in fact, the second-oldest building in Dublin, after the crypt of Christ Church Cathedral. Numerous restorations and rebuilding took place over the centuries, most notably in 1686, and again after the 1922 Civil War. The original keyboard of St Michan's famous 1724 organ is on view in the entrance hall. In 1742 the German composer Handel used this organ on which to practise in preparation for the first ever live performance of his *Messiah* which took place in the Old Musick Hall in Fishamble Street [**30**].

A particular attraction, though not everybody's cup of tea, are the church vaults. The air in these vaults is very dry and the temperature remains constant. According to A.T. Lucas, former Director of the National Museum, 'the church stands on formerly marshy ground and there is a relatively high methane content in the air of the vaults which acts as a preservative'. This rarified atmosphere has kept some of the corpses in the vaults in a semi-mumified condition. Among the partly-preserved bodies in one of the vaults are those of the brothers Henry and John Sheares, both United Irishmen and executed in 1798.

Turn right when you leave St Michan's and walk down Church Street to the river, turning right onto Aran Quay. Directly across

Four Courts

the river are three houses which appear somewhat out of place along a quayside which has been so altered by uninspired modern development that it is all but impossible to imagine how fine the Liffey Quays once were. The three houses – T.P. Nolan, The Creamery and Oifig an Poist (post office) – are three-storey-over-traditional-style shopfront buildings and provide a clue to the lost architectural heritage along this quayside.

Continue along Arran Quay to St Paul's Catholic Church. The writer and philosopher Edmund Burke was born at number 12 Arran Quay (demolished) in 1729 and lived here until 1750, when he went to live in London. **St Paul's Catholic Church** was built between 1835 and 1837 to the design of architect Patrick Byrne, who designed many post-Catholic Emancipation churches in Dublin. The church, with its Greek Ionic tetrastyle portico, tall tower and copper dome, stands out as a building of some

antiquity and character along these quays.

Walk up Lincoln Lane, beside the church – it was formerly named Pudding Lane and was home in the eighteenth century to a Carmelite convent – and continue for a couple of hundred metres into the cobble-stoned Bow Street. On your left are the buildings of the **Old Jameson Distillery**. Jameson whiskey has been distilled here since 1780. The Jameson family built up the company to become one of the largest in Ireland. In 1966, a merger of John Jameson & Son, John Power & Son and Cork Distilleries Company brought about a new whiskey conglomerate, Irish Distillers. Bushmills Distillery in County Antrim joined the Irish Distillers Group in 1972.

The present Visitor Centre opened to the public in 1997 and replaced the Irish Whiskey Corner. The tour, followed by a 'tasting', is interesting and entertaining.

Old Jameson Distillers

until the late 1800s, when Dublin Corporation moved the market to Prussia Street, off the North Circular Road. Prior to the area becoming a cattle market, it formed part of **Oxmantown Green**. The name Oxmantown is derived from the word Ostmantown, meaning town of the man from the east, the easterners being the Norwegians and Danes who established a large settlement around this area in the ninth and tenth centuries. Oxmantown was a distinctly separate area from the walled city across the river and was used by the Vikings as a secure base away from the main action.

The cobble-stoned rectangle is overlooked by a red-brick chimney, built in 1895 by the John Jameson Distillery. In the mid-1960s, Smithfield, for a brief period, became 'Checkpoint Charlie', the East/West Berlin border crossing, for the filming of *The Spy Who Came in from the Cold*, starring Richard Burton and Claire Bloom.

The entire area around here – comprising much more than Smithfield – has recently been designated a 'tax incentive area' and massive redevelopment is expected over the coming years. Certainly, the area urgently needs regeneration, such is the extent of the dereliction caused by a lengthy period of neglect. Explore in your own time the open space, before branching off into Arran Quay Terrace, which leaves Smithfield at the south-western (Liffey end, opposite side) corner.

*[Ten-minute optional diversion: Continue past the entrance to the Visitor Centre for a hundred metres until you reach the rear of the church of* **St Mary of the Angels***. Go through the gates and around to the front, which faces onto Church Street. The interior is worth a visit, not least for the interesting side chapel which, unusually, runs the length of the main church. Retrace your steps.]*

From the entrance to the Visitor Centre, go back down Bow Street and take the first right into New Church Street (not marked). Walk to the end, onto the large open space which is **Smithfield**.

Smithfield was developed as an enclosed cattle market in the late 1600s and retained its place as Dublin's principal cattle market

When you reach the end of the terrace, look left down Queen

Street to the hump of **Liam Mellowes Bridge**, more commonly known as Queen Street Bridge. For a time it was named Queen Maeve Bridge, after the pre-Christian Queen Maeve of Connacht. Built in 1768, it is the oldest existing bridge across the Liffey in Dublin.

Cross Queen Street and walk along Benburb Street for 200 m to the junction with Blackhall Place. Look left to a house directly across the Liffey. The exterior of the house was used in all the outdoor scenes in the American director John Huston's marvellous film of James Joyce's short story *The Dead*. The dark brown-painted house is derelict as I write and its future seems bleak [**80**].

Turn right and walk up Blackhall Place for about 150 m. Set back from the street on the left is the former home of the **Bluecoat School**, also known as King's Hospital School. The present Palladian building was designed by Thomas Ivory and completed in 1783 and, when the school moved to another location in 1970, the **Incorporated Law Society** moved in. Prior to construction, the Bluecoat School was housed in another building on this site (the school was founded in 1669). It was in that original but now demolished building that the Irish Parliament met in 1729, before moving to their magnificent home on College Green (now the Bank of Ireland). The proper name of the school was the Hospital and Free School of King Charles II. That particular mouthful was put aside for the more obvious and user-friendly *Bluecoat School*, a name derived from the colour of the rather elaborate school uniform worn by the pupils until they were allowed wear a less flamboyant – though still blue – uniform in 1923.

At the rear of the main building is a field which is the last surviving part of Oxmantown Green. Unfortunately, neither the buildings nor the grounds are open to the public.

Retrace your steps to the corner of Benburb Street and Blackhall Place. Turn right and continue along Benburb Street for about 300 m, to the entrance to the **National Museum**, formerly Collins Barracks and, before that, Royal Barracks.

The original Royal Barracks were designed by Thomas Burgh (he also designed the Long Room Library in Trinity College) and built between 1704 and 1706, but they have been substantially altered, even as recently as the late 1990s when the Office of Public Works completed a major transformation of an old and rambling army barracks into the fine museum complex you see today. Before the army moved out in the mid-1990s it was the oldest in-use barracks in the world, with the largest barrack square in Europe. A visit to the Museum warrants at least a couple of hours, so visit it now and continue the tour later or on another day – or come back to the Museum at another time.

Leave the Museum's grounds and look across the river to view a sizeable section of the Guinness Brewery. Go right and continue along Benburb Street, the high stone wall of the old barracks on your right, an unused green field on your left. Part of this field, which is called the Esplanade, was used as an unmarked burial site for many Irish men – and women – killed during the 1798 Rebellion, in which Croppies (United Irishmen insurgents) were principally involved. Many of those taken prisoner in the capital were hanged from some of the Liffey bridges. The ground in which they lie buried is referred to as **Croppies Acre**.

Continue. Somewhere along here, Benburb Street becomes Parkgate Street. At the junction with Temple Street West, cross to the **Croppies Memorial Park** on the left, a remembrance garden to the 1798 insurgents. Walk around the park, keeping the railings on your right. From the fountain on the Liffey side, you can see, across the river, the splendid Heuston Station [**81**] and beyond it the graceful Dr Steevens's Hospital [**81**], now home to the Eastern Health Board.

*[Brief diversion and refreshment stop: If you fancy taking a mid-tour break, this is a good opportunity to do so, visiting one of Dublin's finest and most individual of pubs into the bargain. Cross to the Ashling Hotel and continue for 200 m to* **Ryan's Pub**. *It has four snugs (small compartments with a latched door so you won't be disturbed by those in the main bar) and a beautifully ornate interior. The Scotch granite frontage is particularly handsome. It has had, for as long as I can remember, a well-deserved reputation as an efficiently-run establishment. The splendid interior is always glisteningly clean and the pints of porter ponderingly and perfectly poured.]*

From Croppies Memorial Park, go back to the junction of Parkgate Street and Temple Street West and turn left and walk up the hill. Soon, Temple Street West becomes Arbour Hill. At the top of the hill, swing around to the right. On the opposite corner is a small church, easily missed. It is the Greek Orthodox Church of the Annunciation.

Continue along Arbour Hill, passing some of the most northerly buildings of the old barracks on your right and Arbour Hill prison on your left. After 200 m, enter the church grounds on the left and walk around by the back of the church, to the memorial at the end of the formal gardens. This is the **Arbour Hill Memorial**, where the leaders of the 1916 Easter Rising are buried and where commemorations are held every Easter. The words on the memorial are the text of the Proclamation of Independence, read by Patrick Pearse from the front of the General Post Office on O'Connell Street on Easter Monday 1916.

Continue along Arbour Hill for several hundred metres until you descend to a main junction. Turn left here, into **Stoneybatter** (from Stony Bóthar [stony road]). In ancient times, it was part of Sligh Chualann, one of the five great 'highways' of Ireland. Sligh Chualann stretched from Tara in County Meath to Glendalough in

County Wicklow and crossed the Liffey at Áth Cliath (Ford of the Hurdles), where today the Father Mathew Bridge spans the river. The route of Sligh Chualann is almost two thousand years old.

After a couple of hundred metres, Stoneybatter becomes Manor Street. Number 83, on the left, is the birthplace of the poet **Austin Clarke**. A wall plaque identifies the house. At this point, cross to the opposite side of the street, to the entrance to the sisters of Charity Convent, and walk back down into Stoneybatter. Among the many pubs along here is The Glimmerman, on your left. During the Second World War, men were employed by the Government to patrol stealthily around neighbourhoods at nightfall to check if any household was illegally burning gas to light their house. (Gas was severely rationed at the time.) These men became known as Glimmermen.

Continue to the junction with North Brunswick Street, directly opposite Arbour Hill, and turn left and walk along North Brunswick Street for 400 m to the Victorian red-brick building on the left. This is the Dublin Metropolitan District Court, formerly the **Richmond Surgical Hospital** and founded in 1811, though the building you see today dates from 1900. Immediately after the Richmond, turn left into Morning Star Avenue and walk fifty metres to the now defunct **Hardwicke Fever Hospital** (1803), on the right, and the **Whitworth Medical Hospital** (1817), on the

left. They have been converted recently into apartments and offices, respectively. The three hospital buildings were designed by the Georgian architect, Francis Johnston.

Return to North Brunswick Street and turn left, passing Carmichael House on your left. The building, which dates from 1864, is owned by the Eastern Health Board and houses about forty voluntary organisations. Continue to the end of North Brunswick Street and cross at the lights in front of you to the far side, turning right then immediately left into North King Street. The area around here was one of the major battlegrounds during the Easter Rising of 1916.

Walk along North King Street and take the third turning right – after about 250 m – into Halston Street. **Green Street Courthouse**, built in 1790 and designed by Thomas Cooley (he designed the Royal Exchange, now City Hall) is on the left. Used today as the Central Criminal Court, in times past the trials of Henry and John Sheares in 1798 (both of whom are buried in St Michan's Protestant Church vaults), Robert Emmet (1803), the Young Irelanders (1848), the Fenians (1867) and the 'Invincibles' (1883) all took place in this building. Emmet's trial and his speech from the dock are the stuff of legend. He gripped the bar of the dock as he uttered his closing words: *'When my country has taken her place among the nations of the earth, then, and not till then, let my epitaph be written.'* The bar is still in the

Smithfield

courthouse, preserved in a glass showcase. Beside the courthouse is the long defunct Sheriff's Prison, built in 1794.

Across the street from the courthouse is **St Michan's Catholic Church**, completed in 1893 and more commonly known as Halston Street church. It is a quiet and intimate place of worship. Cross to the small public park opposite the church. The park was laid out on the site of **Newgate Prison**, where many political prisoners died, among them the Sheares brothers, and Lord Edward Fitzgerald and Oliver Bond, principals in the 1798 rebellion. The prison was designed by Thomas Cooley and opened in 1780. For the first thirty years of its functioning as a place of incarceration, it was a chamber of horrors. It had a chilling reputation as a prison where murder, rape, violent assault and routine thievery were regarded as the norm in an institution out of control. An 1810

Act of Parliament brought the worst horrors to an end. Newgate ceased to function as a prison in 1863 and, thirty years later, was demolished. A monument to its political prisoners – with a fiercely passionate inscription – is in the park.

If the park is open, go through, onto Green Street. *(If it is closed, go right from the church to the end of the park, onto Little Britain Street.)* Cross the street and go left for twenty metres to view Cooley's Courthouse from this side. Retrace your footsteps to the end of the park and turn right. This is Little Britain Street. Arthur Griffith, founder of Sinn Féin and the United Irishman newspaper and signatory to the Treaty of 1921, was born in this street in 1871. Joycean enthusiasts will know also that Barney Kiernan's pub, in which the Cyclops episode of *Ulysses* was set, was number 8 on this street, now demolished.

Continue in a straight line into

the narrow Cuckoo Lane *(if the park was closed and you've arrived onto Little Britain Street from the church, turn right into Cuckoo Lane)* and turn left into George's Hill. The Presentation Convent National School is on your left, the convent being one of Dublin's oldest. When it opened in 1794 it was the first Catholic school to do so, following the repeal of a law outlawing Catholic schools. Near here, an underground tunnel is said to exist, travelling underneath the Liffey to Christ Church. Perhaps careful excavation and archaeological examination sometime in the future will reveal its existence.

At the end of George's Hill, 150 m along, is one of the entrances to the Dublin Corporation **Fruit, Vegetable and Flower Market**, diagonally left across the street. The Market was established here in 1892. Go left along Mary's Lane and, after a hundred metres, turn right into Arran Street East, keeping the Market on your right. Turn left after 150 m into Mary's Abbey and left again after fifty metres into **Meetinghouse Lane**. The name Meetinghouse Lane has its origins in the house at number 12 (now demolished), formerly the first premises of the Bank of Ireland, before that institution moved to its present location on College Green. When the bank moved, an anti-burgher sect used the building to hold regular meetings, hence the name.

Near the end of the lane on the right is the entrance to the chapter-house remains of the twelfth-century Cistercian **St Mary's Abbey**, one of the largest and most important medieval monasteries in Ireland until its dissolution in 1539 by Henry VIII. At the height of its influence, the abbey was the wealthiest monastery in Ireland, its lands stretching from modern day Ballybough in the east to Grangegorman in the west. The extensive buildings of the abbey took in parts of present-day Capel Street, Little Mary Street, East Arran Street and Mary's Abbey, and its cemetery was situated around where is now the Green Street/North King Street area.

Dating from 1180, the chapter-house is beneath an eighteenth-century warehouse and is where the monks used to gather after morning mass. The chapter-house was also used for political meetings and, in 1534, Lord Silken Thomas Fitzgerald renounced his allegiance to Henry VIII in this building. His rebellion was short lived and he was executed soon after at Tyburn. The chapter-house remains are open to the public, however opening times are very restrictive.

Back on Mary's Abbey, turn left and walk to the junction with Capel Street. To finish the tour, continue in a straight line across Capel Street into Abbey Street Upper and walk all the way to O'Connell Street, less than half-a-kilometre away or, turn right into Capel Street and walk to the river, from where you can either walk left along the quays to O'Connell Bridge, or cross Grattan Bridge to Parliament Street and cut through Temple Bar.

## Three Literary Tours

Dublin boasts a star-studded cast of writers, and they have left a profound collective mark on the city in which they lived, worked, ate, drank and, in many cases, left.

As there are too many fine writers to include in one tour, I have devised three tours of between two and two-and-a-half hours each. Begin where you like, because each tour commences where the previous one ended. The three tours can be undertaken and completed in one session (reserve a day and bring your most comfortable shoes!). Alternatively, you can complete one, even two, and pick up where you left off the next day – or indeed the following year!

*A word of advice: bring a copy of Joyce's 'Dubliners' and one other book by a different Dublin author, to dip into along the way.*

### LITERARY TOUR A — PALACE BAR TO THE SHELBOURNE HOTEL

The tour covers much of the south inner city, beginning near O'Connell Bridge, travelling west as far as St Patrick's Cathedral, diverting south to George Bernard Shaw's birthplace, before heading for the Shelbourne Hotel by way of the Grand Canal. Along the way you will encounter Jonathan Swift, Shaw, Patrick Kavanagh, Elizabeth Bowen and many other writers.

**Tour begins:** *at the Palace Bar on Fleet Street.*

The Palace Bar [**142**] is one of Dublin's literary landmarks. It was a favourite meeting place for writers and journalists in bygone days. The poets **Austin Clarke**, **Patrick Kavanagh**, **John Betjeman** and **F.R. Higgins** all drank and socialised here during the heady days – and nights – of the Irish Literary Revival in the late thirties and early forties. They were invariably joined by the Editor of The Irish Times, **R.M. Smyllie**, a larger than life character in Dublin literary and social circles at the time. **Brian O'Nolan** (pseudonyms **Flann**

### Opening Times

- **St Patrick's Cathedral**
  Telephone (01) 475 4817
  Mon–Fri 9am–6pm
  Saturday 9am–5pm
  Sunday April–September:
  9.30am–11am; 12.45pm–3pm;
  4.15pm–6pm
  October–March: 10am–11am;
  12.45pm–3pm
- **Shaw House**
  Telephone (01) 475 0854
  <u>May–October</u>
  Mon–Sat 10am–5pm
  Sunday/Public Holidays
  11am–5pm
  Closed lunchtime 1pm–2pm
  <u>November–April</u>
  Open only by prior arrangement

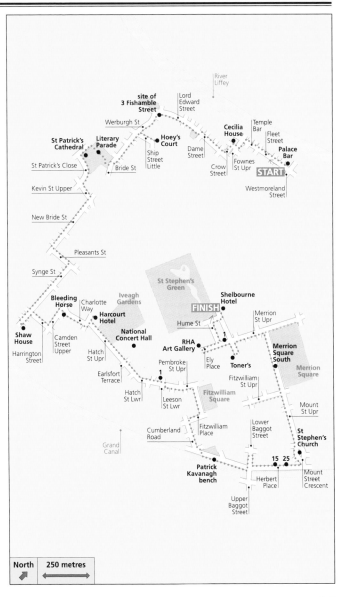

## Tour Facts

- **Length of tour:** 4.8 miles (7.7 kilometres)
- **Duration of tour:** a leisurely 2½ hours
- **Refreshments:** during the tour (the Harcourt Hotel); after the tour (Shelbourne Hotel or O'Donoghue's pub on Merrion Row)
- **Getting to the Starting Point:** from O'Connell Bridge (walk south, towards Trinity College along the right side of Westmoreland Street, turn right immediately after Bewley's Oriental Café into Fleet Street. The Palace Bar is on your immediate right); from Trinity College front gates (turn right outside the gates and walk for a hundred metres and cross to the pedestrian island and cross again to the left to the House of Lords entrance to the Bank of Ireland. Turn right and walk along Westmoreland Street. Take the first left into Fleet Street. The Palace Bar is on your immediate right)
- **Special Note for Walkers:** this is the longest of the three tours. The stretch from St Patrick's Cathedral to the Shaw House is pleasant but off the beaten track, as is the journey from the Shaw House to Harcourt Street.

O'Brien and **Myles na Gopaleen**) also drank here in the forties and fifties.

Continue along Fleet Street and into the heart of Temple Bar. At the far end of Temple Bar Square go left into Fownes Street Upper and turn right into Cecilia Street. Mid-way along Cecilia Street on the right is Cecilia House [**27**], formerly the Medical School of the Catholic University and where **Oliver St John Gogarty** and **James Joyce** studied, Joyce for a shorter period than Gogarty as his father could not afford the fees. Gogarty qualified as a surgeon.

At right angles to Cecilia House is Crow Street. Walk to the top and turn right into Dame Street. At the Olympia Theatre, cross to the opposite side of the street. The entrance to the Lower Castle Yard of Dublin Castle is straight ahead. The novelist **Bram Stoker** [**112**] worked for a brief period in the early 1870s as a civil servant in the Castle. Continue along Dame Street, past on your left City Hall [**42**], the entrance to the Upper Castle Yard of the Castle, and proceed up Lord Edward Street. Turn left at the top. The Castle Inn stands on the site of number 3 Fishamble Street (this section of the street is now named Christchurch Place), birthplace of the poet **James Clarence Mangan** (1803-49). The house was demolished in 1944. Of all the Dublin writers who achieved recognition, either during his lifetime or posthumously, Mangan's life was undoubtedly the most epic in terms of its wretched poverty. His thoroughly dreadful childhood set the scene on what was to descend into a daily struggle to exist throughout his relatively short life. Yet, despite this burden, his artistic spirit survived and he produced some truly memorable songs and ballads, among them

*Dark Rosaleen, The Nameless One* and *Lament for Kincora*.

Continue into Werburgh Street, go past St Werburgh's Church [**70**], and turn left after 150 m into Little Ship Street. This cobblestoned street leads down to Ship Street Gate and another entrance to Dublin Castle. Beside the Castle entrance, a wall plaque at the foot of the Castle Steps marks the approximate location of Hoey's Court, birthplace of **Jonathan Swift**. Hoey's Court is long since demolished. In the Birmingham Tower, just inside Ship Street Gate, the **Austin Clarke Library** (phone 671 4632 for an appointment) commemorates the Dublin-born poet.

Retrace your steps to Werburgh Street and turn left. The next street on the left is Chancery Lane, where **James Clarence Mangan** lived in dire poverty with his family. The house has been demolished. Continue along Werburgh Street and onto Bride Street, passing the fine Victorian Iveagh Buildings [**68**] on your right and the attractive, new Dublin Corporation housing development on your left. Note the interesting circular carvings on the façades – they depict scenes from Swift's *Gulliver's Travels*.

When you reach the park, cross to the right and, keeping the railings on your right, walk to the entrance gate a hundred metres along. Go through the entrance,

St Patrick's Cathedral and Park

into **St Patrick's Park** [**69**]. Walk down the slope – or steps – in front of the gardener's lodge and turn immediately right to **Literary Parade**, erected during Dublin's Millennium year in 1988. The eleven writers originally commemorated are: Jonathan Swift, James Clarence Mangan, Oscar Wilde, George Bernard Shaw, William Butler Yeats, John Millington Synge, Seán O'Casey, James Joyce, Brendan Behan, Austin Clarke and Samuel Beckett. A twelfth has been added recently, that of novelist Eilís Dillon, though why this writer and not, say, Elizabeth Bowen, was chosen is unclear. Walk along the park's main avenue and exit beside the cathedral at the west side. Turn left and left again and visit **St Patrick's Cathedral** [**69**].

Apart from Swift, who dominates any literary references

Shelbourne Hotel

to St Patrick's Cathedral, four other writers deserve to be mentioned. **Douglas Hyde** (1860-1949) was the first President of Ireland (1938-45) and a noted poet, folklorist and a significant contributor to the preservation of the Irish language. He founded the Gaelic League in 1893 and was the first playwright to have a play staged in the Irish language – at the Gaiety Theatre in 1901. A funeral service was held in St Patrick's before his body was brought to its resting place in

**Jonathan Swift** (1667-1745) is buried in the cathedral. He was born at nearby Hoey's Court (seen earlier) on 30 November 1667. Educated at Kilkenny College and later at Trinity College, he was appointed secretary to the statesman, Sir William Temple, at Moor Park in Surrey, England in 1689. Five years later, he took holy orders and left Moor Park briefly to become prebend of Kilroot in County Antrim. He returned to Moor Park in 1696 and remained there until 1699. One of his duties was tutor to Hester Johnson (Stella), a beautiful young woman for whom he held a deep affection throughout his life.

In 1701 he received his doctor's degree from Trinity College and for the next twelve years he spent his time between Dublin and London, active in politics and writing satirical pamphlets directed against the government of the day.

He was bitterly disappointed when, in 1713, he was appointed as Dean of St Patrick's Cathedral. Dublin was then a backwater and he regarded the appointment as nothing less than banishment from where the real action was taking place, London. But Dublin was changing, and Swift quickly grew to use his position to launch further satirical missiles at the British government. He became increasingly incensed at the ill-treatment of Ireland under English rule. His first pamphlet on Irish affairs, published in 1720, advocated boycotting English fabrics. In his anonymous *Drapier's Letters* (1724), he opposed 'Wood's halfpence', a corrupt currency. *A Modest Proposal* (1729) suggested feeding impoverished children to the rich.

His best known book, *Gulliver's Travels*, was published in 1726. It was an overnight success and, unexpectedly and ironically, the voyage to Lilliput became a children's classic. When Stella died in 1728, Swift was sixty. His remaining years were dominated by infirmity and loneliness and he died on 19 October 1745. He is buried beside Stella, inside the present entrance to the cathedral.

County Roscommon. A wall plaque inside the south face of the cathedral is dedicated to him.

The Dublin-born playwright **Denis Johnston** (1901-84) is buried in the Close of the cathedral. The novelist, songwriter, poet and painter **Samuel Lover** (1797-1868) is commemorated by a wall plaque. And the playwright and theatre director **Lennox Robinson** (1886-1958), who was closely associated with the Abbey Theatre for much of his life, is buried in the grounds.

Turn left on leaving the cathedral and walk past the old cemetery and Marsh's Library [69]

on your left, and the Boys' Grammar School and Choir and the Deanery on your right. Turn left at the end of St Patrick's Close into Kevin Street Upper and walk to the junction.

Cross to the right (take care – there are no pedestrian lights here) and continue up New Bride Street and onto Heytesbury Street. Take a left past the former Meath Hospital on your right – where **Brendan Behan** [108] passed away – into Pleasants Street. Take the first right into Synge Street. After the first junction, you will pass the Christian Brothers School on the right, where **Brian O'Nolan** was a pupil until the

**George Bernard Shaw**, the only son of an unsuccessful wholesale merchant, was educated at Wesley College in Dublin. In 1872 Mrs Shaw, a fine mezzo-soprano, left her drinking husband and went to London in pursuit of her singing teacher, George Vandaleur Lee, with whom she had lived for several years in Dublin. George Bernard followed her four years later. In London he was converted to socialism and to vegetarianism and joined the Fabian Society, learning the art of public speaking, an art he never tired of during his long life.

Between 1876 and 1885 he laboured with five novels, none of which had any success. In 1885 he became a book reviewer for the *Pall Mall Gazette* and, a year later, music critic for the London paper, *The Star*. Using the pen name of *Corno di Basseto*, he became well known in literary circles. Finally, recognition that he was a writer of some merit came when his play, *The Devil's Disciple*, won acclaim in New York in 1897 and earned more than £2,000 in royalties, a sizeable sum in those days. The following year he married Irish-born Charlotte Payne-Townsend and, shortly after, settled down to write in a prolific manner, producing on average one new play every year.

Shaw himself considered *Heartbreak House*, produced in New York in 1920, to be his best play. He was awarded the Nobel Prize for Literature in 1925 and, in 1928, he returned to political writing with *The Intelligent Woman's Guide to Socialism and Capitalism*. After the death of his wife in 1943, the seven remaining years of his life were quiet and solitary and he died on 2 November 1950, leaving in his will one-third of the royalties from his published works to the National Gallery of Ireland.

family moved to the coastal suburb of Blackrock in 1927.

Staying on Synge Street, cross Harrington Street and proceed to number 33, on your left. This is the birthplace, on 26 July 1856, of **George Bernard Shaw** (the address at the time was 3 Upper Synge Street). The modest terraced house was built in 1838 and had already been occupied by a number of tenants when the Shaw family moved in in 1852. They remained here until 1866. The house is today in the hands of the Shaw Birthplace Museum Trust and has been restored and furnished to replicate in as far as was possible the actual house in which the Shaw family lived.

Retrace your steps to Harrington Street. Cross to the opposite side, turn right and walk to the main junction. Turn left into Camden Street and walk to the pedestrian lights opposite the Bleeding Horse Pub, an establishment frequented by **James Clarence Mangan** and featured in **James Joyce's** *Ulysses*. The completely refurbished pub you see today bears absolutely no resemblance whatsoever to the Bleeding Horse of either Mangan's or Joyce's Dublin days – or nights.

Cross to the pub and walk along Charlotte Way. The building diagonally to your right when you reach the end was once a busy railway station on the long-defunct Harcourt Street Railway Line, which serviced the suburbs of south Dublin until its closure in 1959. Turn left and walk to the Harcourt Hotel, fifty metres down on the right. Before the building

became a hotel, **Shaw** lived here with his father (his mother had already departed for London) from 1874-6. His next address was to be in London.

Go back up Harcourt Street for a few metres and turn left into Hatch Street. The high wall running along the left side of Hatch Street is the perimeter wall of Iveagh Gardens [**38**]. At the traffic lights, look left down Earlsfort Terrace. The large building on the left is the National Concert Hall. In a previous incarnation, this building housed University College Dublin (UCD) between 1914 and the early 1960s. **Brian O'Nolan** [**109**] studied Irish, English and German here. O'Nolan was a brilliant student and an equally brilliant debater in the Literary and Historical Debating Society of the College. A radical and controversial plan moved the entire university, lock, stock and barrel, to the southern suburbs of Belfield in the 1960s.

Continue through the junction into Hatch Street Lower. Number 1, at the junction with Lower Leeson Street, was the temporary boyhood residence of **George Bernard Shaw** when his mother shared the house with George Vandaleur Lee in 1864. From here they moved, with Lee, to Torca Cottage in Dalkey, in 1866.

Cross Leeson Street and walk along the right side of Pembroke Street Upper. The Focus Theatre, one of the great survivors of Dublin theatre, is hidden away at the end of Pembroke Place on the right. Continue to Fitzwilliam Square. **William Butler Yeats** [**110**] lived in a top-storey apartment at number 42 in the early 1930s. Turn right into Fitzwilliam Square South and right again at the end into Fitzwilliam Place. W.B.'s brother, the painter **Jack B. Yeats**, lived and worked in number 18 on your immediate right. Take the first left into Cumberland Road and proceed to the banks of the Grand Canal. Go left and walk along the canal bank.

Soon you will arrive at a life-sized sculpture in bronze of the poet **Patrick Kavanagh** (1904-67), seated on a bronze bench.

At the lock gates, look across the water to the Kavanagh commemorative seat on the opposite bank, erected by his friends on St Patrick's Day 1968. On this side, beside the lock, is

Patrick Kavanagh

**Patrick Kavanagh** was born in Inniskeen, Co. Monaghan and began writing poetry while in his teens, working on the family farm. In Dublin, he moved from address to address, and apart from a relatively lengthy period between 1946 and 1958 at number 62 Pembroke Road in Ballsbridge, not far from here, he never settled for long in one place. He did remain faithful, however, to the area of the city around Ballsbridge and the Grand Canal and wrote lovingly and lyrically of the area.

Take a seat – and a well-deserved rest – beside the poet and reflect on these lines from one of his best known poems:
*'O Commemorate me where there is water,*
*Canal water, preferably, so stilly*
*Greeny at the heart of summer.'*

another commemorative seat, erected in memory of the songwriter and entertainer **Percy French**.

Continue to Baggot Street Bridge and look right and across the bridge to Upper Baggot Street. This was where Kavanagh spent many of his Dublin years, in and out of different addresses, in and out of local pubs, and spending many hours in Parson's Bookshop on the bridge (recently changed ownership and no longer a bookshop). Before continuing along the canal, go left onto Lower Baggot Street and cross to the opposite side fifty metres down. At number 67, a stone profile on the wall of the poet and nationalist **Thomas Davis** (1814-45) marks the house in which he died of scarlet fever. Davis, assisted by John Blake Dillon and Charles Gavan Duffy, founded the influential *Nation* in 1842, a weekly newspaper which acted as the voice of the Young Irelanders, a nationalist movement led by the

**103**

Oliver Goldsmith outside Trinity

same three men. Return to the canal and turn left and walk along Herbert Place to number 15.

**Brian O'Nolan** lived in the O'Nolan family home at number 25 Herbert Place when he was a young boy and teenager.

Turn left into Mount Street Crescent. The lovely St Stephen's Church [**50**] is better known as the Peppercannister Church. **Percy French** was married here in 1890 and, in 1957, the funeral service for the painter **Jack B. Yeats** took place in the church. **Brendan Behan** lived in number 44 Herbert Street (demolished), the next street on your left, in the mid-1950s. Go straight, into Upper Mount Street. **Patrick Kavanagh** lived in number 37, on the left, for a brief period in late 1963 and early 1964. The English Poet Laureate **John Betjeman** had his office at number 50 when he was working as Press Attaché for the

The Anglo-Irish novelist **Elizabeth Bowen** (1899-1973) was born at number 15 Herbert Place on 7 June 1899. She spent her first seven winters here and throughout her life retained the fondest memories of the house and the neighbourhood. The family's ancestral home, where they spent their summers, was Bowen's Court in Kildorrery, Co. Cork. When Elizabeth was seven, her father became seriously ill and, while he was recovering, her mother took her to England. Six years later, when she was only thirteen, her mother died and she went to live with her aunt in Harpenden in England. She spent most of her summers, however, in Bowen's Court. In 1918 she moved to London and became acquainted with many of the leading writers of the day, including Virginia Woolf and E.M. Forster. Her father died in 1930 and she inherited Bowen's Court, spending as much time there as she could. In 1959, due to financial difficulties, she sold Bowen's Court, which was subsequently demolished.

During her adult life Bowen wrote prolifically, producing ten novels and almost eighty short stories. Her reputation has grown in recent years and she is increasingly regarded as among Ireland's most gifted novelists. She died in London in 1973 and is buried near Bowen's Court.

British Embassy in Dublin, between 1941 and 1943. At the next junction, Merrion Square is in front of you.

*[Short optional diversion: Away to your left, at the junction of Baggot Street and Fitzwilliam Street, number 3 Upper Fitzwilliam Street, on the corner, is the United Arts Club, where writers, painters and musicians have gathered over the years. Its members have included **William Butler Yeats**, **Lennox Robinson** and **Percy French**.]*

Cross and walk along Merrion Square South. Wall plaques mark the houses in which **Joseph Sheridan le Fanu** (70) and **William Butler Yeats** (82 – from 1922 to 1928) lived, and where **AE (George Russell)** (84) worked.

*[Diversion: Tour B passes by the National Gallery (to your right along Merrion Square West), with George Bernard Shaw associations, and by Oscar Wilde's family home and recently unveiled statue (at the junction of Merrion Square West and North. Turn to pages 113-15 if you wish to include these two locations on this tour.]*

Turn left at the end of Merrion Square South and walk past the hundred-metre-long Government Buildings [**50**] on your right to the junction of Merrion Street and Baggot Street. Go left for fifty metres and stop opposite Toner's, a pub with an unusual literary claim to fame, for it was here that **William Butler Yeats** had his one and only drink in a Dublin pub [**151**].

Retrace your steps and go left

into Ely Place. The corner house on the left (the door is blocked off) was formerly number 1 Ely Place and it was in this house that **Oscar Wilde** proposed, successfully, to Constance Lloyd. Near the end of the street, on Ely Place Upper, **Oliver St John Gogarty** lived in a house where now stands the Royal Hibernian Academy Art Gallery. Directly opposite the RHA Gallery, **AE (George Russell)** lived in number 3 and his friend, the novelist **George Moore**, lived in number 4.

Returning along Ely Place Upper, turn left into Hume Street. Facing you is the eastern side of St Stephen's Green. Turn right at the end of the street and walk towards the Shelbourne Hotel, stopping to look at the wall plaque on number 33, just beside the hotel. **Gogarty** rented consulting rooms here between 1915 and 1917.

**George Moore** spent the winter of 1883-4 in the Shelbourne, while **Elizabeth Bowen** wrote about the hotel as follows:

*'Celebrities frequented it, local genius did not despise its halls. Bright-plumaged guests from across the water mingled with Irish country families come to town.'*

If you are a celebrity, a local genius, a bright-plumaged guest or a member of an Irish country family – even if you are none of these – treat yourself to a richly-deserved refreshment while you reflect on the great writers you have come across on *Tour A* of Three Literary Tours.

The tour resides in the south inner city. Along the way, you will encounter some of the city's greatest writers, among them James Joyce, Brendan Behan, Brian O'Nolan, William Butler Yeats, Samuel Beckett and Oscar Wilde.

## Tour Facts

- **Length of tour:** 4.2 miles (6.7 kilometres)
- **Duration of tour:** a leisurely 2 hours
- **Refreshments:** during the tour (the National Gallery restaurant; any of the nearby hotels); after the tour (Mulligan's, naturally enough; Harrison's Restaurant on Westmoreland Street for something more substantial; Bewley's Oriental Café on Westmoreland Street for tea and scones)
- **Getting to the Starting Point:** from Trinity front gates (walk left, up Grafton Street, turn left at Marks and Spencers into Duke Street. Davy Byrne's is on your right)

## Opening Times

- **Newman House**
  Telephone (01) 706 7422
  June–August
  Tues–Fri 12pm–5pm
  Saturday 2pm–5pm
  Sunday 11am–2pm
  Closed Monday
  Phone to arrange visiting time during rest of the year
- **National Library**
  Telephone: (01) 661 8811
  Mon–Wed 10am–9pm
  Thurs–Fri 10am–5pm
  Saturday 10am–1pm
  Closed Sunday
- **National Gallery**
  Telephone: (01) 661 5133
  Mon–Sat 10am–5.30pm
  (Thursday till 8.30pm)
  Sunday 2pm–5pm

**Tour begins:** *at the Shelbourne Hotel if you are continuing on from Tour A, or at Davy Byrne's pub on Duke Street, if you are starting from scratch.*

Turn right from the hotel and walk along St Stephen's Green North for a couple of hundred metres. Turn right into Dawson Street, walk past the Mansion House [9] and the Royal Irish Academy [9] next door and turn left opposite St Ann's Church into South Anne Street. At Kehoe's pub [149] go right and walk to the end, turning left into Duke Street. Davy Byrne's is immediately on your left.

**Davy Byrne's [149]** is one of Dublin's most famous literary landmarks. It was here that Leopold Bloom, hero of **James Joyce**'s *Ulysses*, took a light lunch during his fictional odyssey around Dublin on 16 June 1904, the actual day that Joyce walked out with Nora Barnacle in real life (they had met briefly and by chance on Nassau Street a week or so before). In *Ulysses*, Bloom drops in to Davy Byrne's 'moral pub' at lunchtime and has a glass of

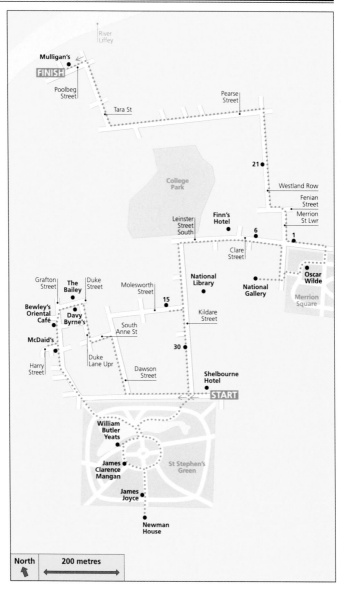

burgundy and a gorgonzola cheese sandwich.

*'Mr Bloom ate his strips of sandwich, fresh clean bread, with relish of disgust, pungent mustard, the feety savour of green cheese. Sips of his wine soothed his palate. Not logwood that. Tastes fuller this weather with the chill off.*

*Nice quiet bar. Nice piece of wood in that counter. Nicely planed. Like the way it curves there.'*

The playwright **Brendan Behan** and novelist and short story writer **Liam O'Flaherty** were regular patrons of the pub.

Across the street, **The Bailey** was a meeting place for many writers, including **Patrick Kavanagh**, **Brendan Behan**, **Brian O'Nolan** and **Oliver St John Gogarty**. Its owner at the time was John Ryan, an editor and publisher and a friend and confidante to many Dublin writers in the fifties and sixties. The door of number 7 Eccles Street, the fictional home of Leopold Bloom, was for many years located in the pub's hallway. Prior to the pub receiving a radical overhaul in recent times, the door was moved to the James Joyce Cultural Institute on North Great George's Street. The Bailey's modern interior bears absolutely no resemblance to the pub of Behan, O'Nolan, Kavanagh and Gogarty's time. Further up the street is The Duke, another of **Brendan Behan** and **Patrick Kavanagh**'s drinking haunts. Whatever character the pub had once, the relatively recent 'restoration' sent it packing.

Go left to Grafton Street and turn left and walk thirty metres to Bewleys Oriental Café **[11]** where, long before the aroma of roasting coffee beans wafted on to the street, Samuel Whyte's Academy stood, providing an education to some pupils who would in later life leave a rich variety of legacies behind them, among them **Thomas Moore**, **Richard Brinsley Sheridan**, **Arthur Wellesley** (who would later become the Duke of Wellington), **George Petrie** and the patriot

---

**Brendan Behan** was born in Holles Street Maternity Hospital on 9 February 1923. During the late 1940s and throughout the 1950s he was a larger than life figure in Dublin. His strong Republican family background and passionate beliefs led to him being arrested in Liverpool for possession of explosives while he was still in his early teens. Back in Dublin, he served five years in Mountjoy Jail, Arbour Hill and the Curragh Army Camp, following an incident after an Easter Rising commemoration in Glasnevin Cemetery. In prison, he became fluent in the Irish language. His writing began to take shape during the fifties and he enjoyed massive success and popularity both at home and abroad with his plays, *The Quare Fellow* and *The Hostage*, and with his autobiography, *Borstal Boy*. He died in 1964 at the age of forty-one, burned out by the drink and a lifestyle which ultimately took its toll on one of Dublin's most colourful literary figures. His funeral to Glasnevin Cemetery was the biggest in Dublin since that of Michael Collins forty-two years earlier.

**Robert Emmet**. Moore and Emmet became close friends while they were attending Whyte's Academy, a friendship which was to come to a shocking and violent end when Emmet was executed in 1803 outside St Catherine's Church in James Street for his leading role in the rebellion of that same year.

Continue up Grafton Street and take the first right into Harry Street. On the left is another famous literary pub, **McDaid's** [**148**]. It was to this pub more than any other that **Brendan Behan**, **Patrick Kavanagh** and **Brian O'Nolan** were drawn.

Return to Grafton Street and continue to where it meets St Stephen's Green. The Gaiety Theatre [**10**] is fifty metres down South King Street on the right. To your left is a fine terrace of mainly eighteenth-century houses. The large building, number 8, with its curved steps and balustrades, is the **Hibernian United Services Club**, built in the 1770s for the Bishop of Killala. Sir Walter Scott stayed overnight in the house in 1825.

Joyce Bust

Across the street is the Fusiliers' Arch, the main gateway to St Stephen's Green [**34**]. Cross and walk through the Arch. Ahead of you is a section of the large ornamental pond which accounts for a significant portion of the northern area of the park. Walk to the water's edge and go left along the lake and turn right onto the

**Brian O'Nolan** (1911-66) wrote his major literary works under the pseudonym Flann O'Brien. He also wrote a thrice-weekly and sharply satirical column for The Irish Times for twenty-five years, under another pseudonym, Myles na gCopaleen. After he graduated from University College Dublin, he took up employment in the Department of Local Government, situated at the time in the Custom House, and remained there for eighteen years, when he was forced to retire due to ill health. During his years in the civil service O'Nolan frequented many drinking establishments around the city, but McDaid's was probably his most regular haunt. In recent years O'Nolan has begun to receive the international recognition he richly deserves. His satirical and comic genius is plainly evident in his novels, *The Poor Mouth*, *At Swim-Two-Birds* and *The Third Policeman*, and in his bizarre and wonderfully crafted regular columns in The Irish Times, available in most bookshops under the title, *The Best of Myles*.

**William Butler Yeats** was born on 13 June 1865 in Sandymount Avenue, about two miles from here. He was the eldest son of John Butler Yeats, a well-known Irish painter. Shortly after his birth, the family moved to London and remained there until 1880. He attended school in Hammersmith but spent his holidays in Sligo where his grandparents, the Pollexfens, were millers and small shipowners.

Back in Dublin, William was sent to the High School, which was then in Harcourt Street. Later, he attended the Metropolitan School of Art, where he became friendly with the writer George Russell (AE) and a group of mystics. One of his first works was *The Wanderings of Oisin*, based on Irish mythology.

In 1889 he met and fell in love with the patriot Maud Gonne, the subject of many of his wonderful love poems. His love for her, which lasted his lifetime, was unrequited – she refused his proposals of marriage in 1891 and again in 1916. However, under her influence, he joined the revolutionary Irish Republican Brotherhood and played, for a time, a prominent part in the organisation.

Yeats was the creator of the Irish Literary Theatre, which had its beginnings in 1899 with the first performance of *The Countess Cathleen*. In 1902 he wrote *Cathleen Ni Houlihan* and asked Maud Gonne to play the lead role. He later became co-director of The Irish National Theatre with Lady Gregory, with premises in the Abbey Theatre [**118**]. He became director in 1906, retaining this role until his death.

In 1917 he married George Hyde-Lees and settled down, devoting his time to writing poetry of sustained brilliance, much of which is included in the volumes *The Wild Swans at Coole* (1919), *The Tower* (1928), and *The Winding Stair* (1933). He had decided, following the trauma of the Easter Rising of 1916, to live full-time in Ireland, and he took up summer residence in a small Norman castle, Thoor Ballylee, in East Galway in 1922. With the birth of the new Irish State in the same year, he was appointed to the Senate and, a year later, was awarded the Nobel Prize for Literature. He died at Roquebrune, overlooking Monaco, on 28 January 1939. His remains were brought back to Ireland for burial 'under bare Ben Bulben's head' in north County Sligo.

'Under bare Ben Bulben's head
   In Drumcliff churchyard Yeats is laid.
   An ancestor was rector there
   Long years ago, a church stands near,
   By the road an ancient cross.
   No marble, no conventional phrase;
On limestone quarried near the spot
   By his command these words are cut:
   Cast a cold eye
   On life, on death.
   Horseman, pass by!'
From *Under Ben Bulben*

bridge. Descend to the central, circular gardens. Walk right, around the perimeter of this central section, to the pagoda-style rain shelter. Beside the shelter are stone steps which lead up to a clearing in the lush growth. At the far end of the clearing is a statue by Henry Moore of the poet **William Butler Yeats** [**110**], erected in 1967. The sculpture is not signposted, so the area here offers the visitor an unusual haven of tranquillity.

Go back down the steps and continue along the curved path. After ten metres, stop and look at the bust of James Clarence Mangan [**98**], a Dublin poet who

**James Joyce** was born at 41 Brighton Square, Dublin on 2 February 1882, the son of John Stanislaus Joyce, an official in the tax office. The family were relatively well off and moved house frequently, in the early years out of choice, but later due to a rapid decline in John Joyce's financial situation. When he was six, James was sent to board at Clongowes Wood Jesuit College in County Kildare, but had to leave a few years later when his father lost his job. He continued his studies at home, before finally going to Belvedere College in the northern part of the city and later to University College Dublin where he studied languages.

After graduating in 1902, he went to Paris on borrowed money, but with no regular income he came near to destitution. In 1903 he returned to Dublin in response to a telegram from his father informing him about his mother's imminent death. Back in Dublin, he applied unsuccessfully for a job in the National Library. He also took singing lessons and sang at the Antient Concert Rooms (now demolished) on Lombard Street East, on the same programme as John McCormack. During this period he met Oliver St John Gogarty, on whom he modelled the character Buck Mulligan, in the opening scene of *Ulysses*. In a more significant personal encounter, he met and pursued Nora Barnacle, a Galway woman of no financial means who was working in Finn's Hotel on Nassau Street.

In October 1904 he and Nora left Ireland for good. Joyce returned briefly on two occasions: in 1909 to open the Volta Cinema in Mary Street, a business venture that failed soon after opening; and in 1912, to arrange – unsuccessfully – for publication of his book of short stories, *Dubliners*. James and Nora spent the greater part of the war years in Zurich. Joyce's ongoing financial difficulties were relieved by a grant from the Royal Literary Fund and by a number of extraordinarily generous benefactors. In 1914 *Dubliners* was published, followed in 1916 by *Portrait of the Artist as a Young Man*. *Ulysses* was published in Paris in 1922 and brought international recognition to Joyce. The book was seen as a unique work of art: it changed the form and content of the novel in a way no other book in the entire history of literature has done.

In Paris, Joyce worked for seventeen years on the book he himself regarded as his magnum opus, *Finnegans Wake*, which was published in 1939. He died on 13 January 1941 in Zurich and is buried there.

Oscar lived and died in abject poverty. Continue for twenty metres and turn right and walk along the straight path, past the bandstand. Just before and to the right of the narrow entrance gate directly ahead is a bust of **James Joyce**, by Marjorie Fitzgibbon.

During his years in Dublin, the Joyce family had more than ten addresses. The earlier houses were in the fashionable southern suburbs, the later ones were north of the Liffey and were located in poorer and poorer districts as the family fortunes declined. Unusually, all but two of the houses are still standing.

Leave the Green by the narrow gate at the end of the path and walk right, to the wooden seat which commemorates Dubliner Joyce and his father, Corkonian John Stanislaus Joyce. Now, cross to **Newman House [46]**, the grey, granite building directly across the street. This was the Catholic University of Ireland, where Joyce studied between 1898 and 1902.

**Gerard Manley Hopkins** (1844-89) taught Latin and Greek in Newman House from 1884 until his death.

Retrace your steps through the Green. When you cross back over the small bridge, there are paths going in four directions. Take the one on the extreme right and walk beside the pond. Fifteen metres after the wooden pavilion, go left and exit the park. Cross at the pedestrian lights directly ahead and walk down the left side of Kildare Street.

The author **Bram Stoker** (1847-1912) lived in a top-floor apartment in number 30, two doors down from Schoolhouse Lane. Stoker was born in Clontarf, a north coastal suburb, and was educated in Trinity College. All through his life he maintained a passionate interest in the theatre. Following his marriage to Florence Balcombe in 1878, the couple moved to London, where Stoker became manager of the Lyceum Theatre. In 1898 he published *Dracula*. The rest, as they say, is history.

Continue down Kildare Street and turn left into Molesworth Street. Across the street, at number 15, two doors past the Masonic Hall [**48**], **George Bernard Shaw** [**101**] worked as a cashier in the offices of Land Agents, Messrs Uniacke and Courtney. Shaw was fifteen when he commenced work here. **Elizabeth Bowen** [**104**] attended dancing classes as a child at Molesworth Hall (now demolished).

Return to Kildare Street. Directly opposite are three important buildings, all featured in the South Georgian Tour [**48**]: the National Museum on the right; Leinster House in the centre; and the National Library on the left, where **James Joyce** studied and where he met **Oliver St John Gogarty** in 1902.

Continue to the bottom of Kildare Street. The corner building on the right is a fine Victorian building which housed the Kildare Street Club [**51**], a gentlemen's club founded in 1782. Turn right and walk along Nassau Street. At the end of the Trinity College railings (150 m along) is a terrace of red-brick houses. On the side of the house adjoining the railings you may – depending on the time of year and whether there are leaves on the adjoining lime tree – be able to read the faded words, Finn's Hotel. This was the hotel in

which **Nora Barnacle** worked as a chambermaid. Joyce first saw and met Nora on Nassau Street in early June 1904 and, following this first meeting, he wrote to her from his lodgings on Shelbourne Road, requesting a rendezvous. They did not meet, but Joyce persisted and they walked out together for the first time on 16 June. From then on, their lives were intertwined.

Continue into Clare Street. **Samuel Beckett** lived for a time in the garret of number 6, on the left. Thirty metres further on, on your right, is **Greene's Bookshop**, featured in Beckett's *Dream of Fair to Middling Women*.

Turn right at the junction beyond Greene's into Merrion Square West and walk to the **National Gallery**. As a teenager, **George Bernard Shaw** spent

**Samuel Beckett** was born on Kerrymount Avenue in the south Dublin suburb of Foxrock on 13 April 1906 (the house is still there). He was educated in Dublin and Enniskillen and finally at Trinity College where he graduated with a First in modern literature. In school, he was a superb athlete and won many honours on the sports field, though this physical fitness was not a feature of the rest of his adult life.

After graduating, he travelled in France and met and befriended James Joyce in Paris. He returned to Ireland and received his MA degree, but soon left again for Paris. He was active in the Resistance during the Second World War and narrowly missed capture. In 1945 General de Gaulle presented him with the Croix de Guerre for his work with the Resistance. Soon after, he took up a post of interpreter and storekeeper at the Irish Red Cross hospital in Saint-Lo in Normandy.

Back in Paris in 1946, he began a period of great creativity and productivity. His trilogy of novels, written in French and later translated into English, were published. These were, *Malone Dies*, *Molloy*, and *The Unnameable* and marked Beckett out as an outstanding talent with a truly individual voice. In 1948 he wrote the play for which he is best known, *Waiting for Godot*. In later years many people came from Ireland to visit him, however his life became increasingly reclusive and he rarely gave interviews. In 1969 he won the Nobel Prize for Literature. He died in Paris in December 1989 and is buried in Montparnasse Cemetery.

many afternoons visiting the Gallery and argued later in life that his many afternoons spent here provided him with a more enriching education than any he might have had at university. A fine bronze statue by Paul Troubetzkoy of Shaw can be seen in The Dargan Wing of the Gallery (turn immediately left once inside). Before you leave, walk to Room VI, the last room in the line of rooms facing you when you enter the Gallery, to view some of the paintings of Jack Yeats, brother of W.B.

When you leave the Gallery, cross to the Rutland Fountain [**51**] on the opposite side of the street, turn left and, twenty metres after the fountain, enter Merrion Square through the narrow open gate. Turn left inside the park and walk the few metres to the very fine modern sculpture by Danny Osborne of *Oscar*, sprawled across a rock and looking over at the house in which he lived between 1855 and 1878, number 1 Merrion Square, one of Dublin's most famous literary addresses.

Continue along the path and

**Oscar Wilde** was born on 16 October 1854, the youngest son of the extrovert surgeon and archaeologist Sir William Wilde and his wife, the flamboyant Jane Francesca Elgee, who wrote under the pen name of Speranza. He was educated at Portora Royal School in Enniskillen, Co. Fermanagh (the school which Beckett attended many years later), at Trinity College, Dublin and finally at Magdalen College, Oxford, from which he graduated with first-class honours in classics and the humanities.

In London, Oscar quickly acquired a reputation for his sharp intellect and rapier-like, witty conversation. In 1884 he married Constance Lloyd and began a serious writing career. Four years later, he published *The Happy Prince and Other Tales*, a collection of wonderfully imaginative fairy stories. His only novel, *The Picture of Dorian Gray* (1891), received poor reviews, but his first comedy play, *Lady Windemere's Fan*, produced in London in 1892, was an instant hit. There quickly followed three more plays, all of them hugely successful: *A Woman of No Importance*, *An Ideal Husband*, and *The Importance of Being Earnest*. He was the toast of London, and admired and loved throughout the land.

In 1895 he was arrested and charged with homosexual offences and, in May of the same year, following a trial by jury, was sentenced to two years imprisonment with hard labour. He served most of his sentence in Reading Gaol, worlds away from the life he had created for himself: he later wrote movingly of his time there in *The Ballad of Reading Gaol*, published in 1898. While he was in prison, he was declared a bankrupt and, on his release from prison in May 1897, he left England to spend the rest of his life in exile in Italy and in France, separated from his wife and children, whom he missed terribly. He died of cerebral meningitis at the Hotel d'Alsace in Paris on 30 November 1900 after receiving the last rites of the Catholic church. He is buried in the cemetery of Père Lachaise in Paris.

leave the park through the first gate you come to. Taking extreme care, cross to the far side of the street and go left as far as the Wilde house on the corner, stopping to read the wall plaques to Oscar and his father (why not his mother?) outside the house. Go right into Merrion Street Lower and walk past the Davenport Hotel. At the corner, look right to The Ginger Man pub on the opposite corner, named after J.P. Dunleavy's novel. The pub has no associations with the author. Cross to Fenian Street and walk left, to the corner with Westland Row. Across the street to your left is 'Sweny's Chemist – Druggist', where Leopold Bloom in *Ulysses* bought 'sweet lemony soap' in 1904, cost 4d (old pence).

Turn right into Westland Row. A hundred metres along, on the left, is number 21, birthplace of **Oscar Wilde**. Further along on your right is the Catholic Church of St Andrew (1832-43), where **Brendan Behan** married Beatrice Salkeld in 1955 (and where the author of this walking guide was baptised!). Beside the church is Pearse Station, named after **Patrick Pearse** (1879-1916), a writer and poet, but better known as one of the leaders of the 1916 Easter Rising. He was executed by the British Government on 3 May 1916 for his part in the Rising.

At the end of the street, cross to Mahaffy's pub. Straight ahead is Lombard Street East, on which stood the former Antient Concert Rooms. Ireland's greatest singer, the tenor **John McCormack** (1884-1945), once shared a platform here with a young man

named **James Joyce,** who himself possessed an exquisite tenor voice but was to find his vocation in another discipline. The building was also the venue for the staging of the earliest plays of the Irish Literary Theatre, an organisation founded at the end of the nineteenth century and which was the forerunner of the Abbey Theatre.

Cross to the left at Mahaffy's and walk along Pearse Street. The street was named Great Brunswick Street when the Pearse family lived here, at number 27, several hundred metres along on the right – there is a stone tablet on the first floor façade, with the carved heads of brothers Willie (Liam) and Patrick (Padraig). Between here and number 27 and on the same side of the street is St Mark's Church, founded in 1729 and sold by the Church of Ireland to Trinity College in 1971. In 1985 the building was acquired by St Mark's Family Worship Centre. **Oscar Wilde** was christened in the church on 26 April 1855.

Turn right after the Pearse house into Tara Street and take the second left into Poolbeg Street. Mulligan's pub [**145**], on your right, was one of **Brendan Behan**'s regular watering holes. The pub features in *Counterparts*, one of the stories in **James Joyce**'s *Dubliners*.

*'When the Scotch House closed they went round to Mulligan's. They went into the parlour at the back and O'Halloran ordered small hot specials all round.'*

This tour ends here. If it is a cold, winter's day, small hot specials all round, please!

The tour covers much of the north inner city – including Dublin's principal thoroughfare, O'Connell Street – and ends up in the heart of the south inner city, at Trinity College. Along the way, you will encounter some of the city's greatest writers, among them James Joyce, William Butler Yeats, John Millington Synge, Seán O'Casey, Oliver St John Gogarty, Oliver Goldsmith, Oscar Wilde and Jonathan Swift.

**Tour begins:** *at Mulligan's Pub on Poolbeg Street.*

Mulligan's on Poolbeg Street [**145**] features in *Counterparts*, one of the stories in **James Joyce**'s *Dubliners*.

*'They were all beginning to feel mellow. Farrington was just standing another round when Weathers came back. Much to Farrington's relief he drank a glass of bitter this time. Funds were getting low, but they had enough to keep them going.'*

From *Counterparts*

The pub was one of **Brendan Behan**'s [**108**] regular watering holes.

Go left when you leave the pub and turn left immediately into Tara Street and cross the Liffey at Butt Bridge, straight ahead. When you reach the centre of the bridge, look towards the sea to the twin chimneys of the Electricity Supply Board (ESB) stretching to the sky: they are near the coastal suburb of Sandymount, where William Butler Yeats was born and along which strand Joyce walked during the early days of September 1904, presumably contemplating his imminent departure for Europe with Nora Barnacle. He was staying briefly at an address on Strand Road in Sandymount.

## Tour Facts

- **Length of tour:** 4.2 miles (6.7 kilometres)
- **Duration of tour:** a leisurely 2 hours
- **Refreshments:** during the tour (either the James Joyce Cultural Centre or the Dublin Writers Museum); after the tour (you are in the heart of the south inner city, adjacent to Temple Bar and Grafton Street, so you are spoilt for choice. A few suggestions, nonetheless: Palace Bar on Fleet Street, Bewley's Oriental Café on Westmoreland Street; Harrison's Restaurant opposite Bewley's)
- **Getting to the Starting Point:** from O'Connell Bridge (walk east [towards the sea] along Burgh Quay, take the first right and immediately turn left into Poolbeg Street. Mulligan's is on your left); from Trinity front gates (walk right from the front gates for about three hundred metres. Cross at the pedestrian lights to the Screen Cinema and walk along Hawkins Street [beside the cinema]. Turn right into Poolbeg Street)

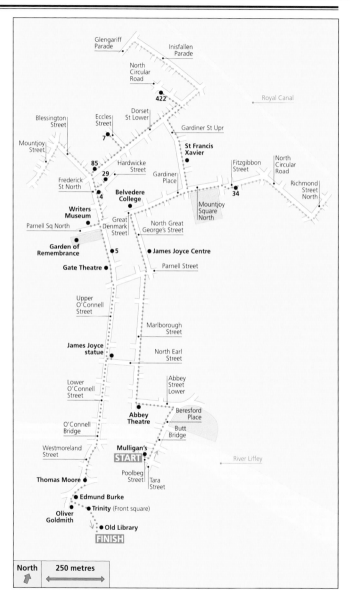

Glengariff Parade

Inisfallen Parade

North Circular Road

422

Blessington Street

Eccles Street

Dorset St Lower

Gardiner St Upr

St Francis Xavier

Mountjoy Street

7

85

Hardwicke Street

29

Gardiner Place

Fitzgibbon Street

North Circular Road

Richmond Street North

34

Frederick St North

4

Belvedere College

Writers Museum

Great Denmark Street

North Great George's Street

Mountjoy Square North

Parnell Sq North

Garden of Remembrance

5

James Joyce Centre

Gate Theatre

Parnell Street

Upper O'Connell Street

Marlborough Street

James Joyce statue

North Earl Street

Lower O'Connell Street

Abbey Street Lower

O'Connell Bridge

Abbey Theatre

Beresford Place

Butt Bridge

Westmoreland Street

Mulligan's
**START**

River Liffey

Thomas Moore

Poolbeg Street

Tara Street

Edmund Burke

Trinity (Front square)

Oliver Goldsmith

Old Library
**FINISH**

North

250 metres

At the far side of the bridge, cross to Liberty Hall, Dublin's tallest office block, and continue in a straight line along Beresford Place. Turn sharp left after less than a hundred metres into Abbey Street Lower. After a few hundred metres you will arrive at the **Peacock** and **Abbey Theatres,** on the corner of Abbey Street and Marlborough Street.

The Abbey Theatre was founded by **Lady Gregory** and **William Butler Yeats** and opened in 1904. Its first stormy controversy burst on stage in 1907 with the rioting which greeted **John Millington Synge**'s *Playboy of the Western World.* The vaguely immoral tone for the time which the play suggested shocked the puritan mind of the mainly Catholic and nationalist audience. Riots again erupted in 1926 when **Seán O'Casey**'s passionate 1916 Easter Rising drama, *The Plough and the Stars*, disgusted the audience with its honest attempt to portray the drama of the Rising. Yeats made his famous speech from the stage immediately the curtain came down. *'You have disgraced yourselves again. Is this to be an ever-recurring celebration of the arrival of Irish genius? Synge first and then O'Casey.'*

In 1951 the original building was destroyed by fire and, in 1966, the present building, designed by Michael Scott, was opened. Happily, there are plans afoot to give the bland building a thorough renewal. The main foyer and stairwell has some interesting portraits of famous Irish theatrical figures and performances.

Take a right into Marlborough Street and walk to the end, passing Tyrone House [21] on your right after a hundred metres and, shortly after, the Pro-Cathedral [20] on your left. The area around here once formed part of 'Monto', after Montgomery Street. It was a notorious brothel quarter and features in the 'Circe' chapter in *Ulysses*. Most of the brothels were raided and closed down in 1924, due to the vigilance of the Legion of Mary, under Frank Duff.

At the end of Marlborough Street, cross Parnell Street and go up North Great George's Street [59]. The poet **Samuel Ferguson** (1810-86) lived in number 20 for exactly half his life. His house was a fulcrum of intellectual and social activity during much of his time here, and many literary gatherings took place in the house. Across the street, number 35 is the **James Joyce Cultural Centre**, opened in 1994. It is an essential visit for any Joyce enthusiast. The Joycean scholar Senator David Norris, who lives across the street in a restored period house, was and remains one of the driving forces behind the project. Three doors up from the Joyce Centre is number 38, where John Pentland Mahaffy, scholar, wit and Provost of Trinity College between 1914 and 1919, lived.

Walk to the top of the street. Facing you is Belvedere House [**58**], standing on Great Denmark Street. Lord Belvedere's house was begun in 1775 and is today occupied by a Jesuit school for boys, Belvedere College. **James Joyce** attended school here 1893-8, and it is featured in *Portrait of the Artist as a Young Man*. The poet **Austin Clarke** was also a pupil here.

Turn right into Great Denmark Street and walk through Gardiner Place to Mountjoy Square [**57**]. No need to walk around the square, unless you wish to see number 53 (located at the end of the terrace to your right) where **William Butler Yeats** had occasional lodgings, and/or number 35 (located in the middle of Mountjoy Square South, diagonally right from the corner on which you are standing), where the playwright **Seán O'Casey** lived for a brief period (the original house was demolished and has been replaced by a modern pastiche replica). O'Casey's play, *The Shadow of a Gunman*, was probably set here.

From your location at the corner of Great Denmark Street and Mountjoy Square, continue in a straight line along Mountjoy Square North and, at the end, cross and walk along Fitzgibbon Street for thirty metres. Number 34, on your right, was the **Joyce** family home for one year in the early 1890s (at the time, the address was 14 Fitzgibbon Street). Although the street has very few original houses left, it was at the time a fashionable address in the north inner city and it was to be the last of the Joyces' 'good' addresses before they began their social and financial decline.

*[Diversion: If you wish to see another Joyce house, continue to the end of Fitzgibbon Street and turn right into North Circular Road. North Richmond Street is on the left. The Joyce family – all twelve of them – lived in number 17 for four years from 1895.]*

From Fitzgibbon Street, retrace your footsteps back along Mountjoy Square North and turn right into Gardiner Street Upper. Walk to St Francis Xavier Church [**58**], on the right. The church is featured at the end of **James Joyce**'s short story, *Grace*. Continue to the traffic lights. Dorset Street runs left and right along here. The playwright **Richard Brinsley Sheridan** (1751-1816) was born at number 12 Dorset Street.

Turn right and take the first left into North Circular Road. **Seán O'Casey** lived in number 422, a hundred metres up on the left, between 1918 and 1926. This is where he wrote his finest plays: *The Shadow of a Gunman* (1923),

**119**

*Juno and the Paycock* (1924) and *The Plough and the Stars* (1926). *[Twenty minute optional diversion: Rejoin Dorset Street and take the next left into Innisfallen Parade, where O'Casey lived as a young boy, in* number 9. *Mountjoy Jail, where Brendan Behan spent time behind bars, backs onto Innisfallen Parade. Behan wrote his first play, 'The Landlady', in the 'Joy. Innisfallen Parade leads onto Glengariff Parade, where the*

**Seán O'Casey** was born at 85 Dorset Street Upper (you will pass the site of the house shortly) on 30 March 1880. He was the youngest of thirteen children and one of five who did not succumb to croup, a common disease at the time. Only himself, three brothers and a sister survived infancy.

His parents were relatively poor Protestants. When Seán was six, his father died and he went to live with his mother and his older sister Bella in a two-roomed attic in 20 Lower Dominick Street, a house today renowned for its remarkable stuccoed hallway and ceilings, but whose stuccoed walls and ceilings were understandably not high on the list of priorities for the troubled O'Caseys.

At the age of fourteen, Seán began to earn a living. For the next thirty years he would work mostly as a labourer, spending nine of those years working on the railroad. He changed address a few more times, eventually arriving at 422 North Circular Road in 1918, following the death of his mother that same year.

O'Casey was a self-educated man. He consumed books, despite an eye ailment that caused him severe difficulty throughout his life. His writings reflect his interest over the years in the trade union movement (one of the greatest influences in his life was that of the trade unionist leader Jim Larkin [**18**]), the Irish language, and the Irish Citizen Army, of which he was Secretary. This organisation had been formed by Larkin in 1914, following the previous year's general strike. Two years later, it was to play a significant role in the Easter Rising.

O'Casey began writing and, in 1923, *The Shadow of a Gunman* was performed at the Abbey, followed by *Juno and the Paycock* a year later and *The Plough and the Stars* in 1926. Despite the riots which greeted the latter, O'Casey had established himself as a playwright with a distinctive voice and a willingness to tackle the most sensitive Irish subjects.

In 1926 he left for London, having decided to become a full-time writer. He married the actress Eileen Carey the following year. He was soon to discover that life as a writer was not going to be easy: the Abbey rejected his next play, *The Silver Tassie*. He was not to know it at the time, but he had already reached the pinnacle of his creativity and of his success. Despite a significant output, none of his plays came near to the power of the first three. *I Knock at the Door*, the first of a six-volume autobiography, was published in 1939. The final volume, *Sunset and Evening Star* appeared in 1954. O'Casey died in Torquay on 18 September 1964.

*Joyce family lived at number 32 in 1901-2.]*

From number 422 North Circular Road, rejoin Dorset Street and turn right and walk a relatively uninteresting 400 m to Eccles Street, on the right. Go fifty metres up Eccles Street and stop at the entrance to the Mater Private Hospital. A wall plaque marks the location of number **7 Eccles Street**, one of Dublin's most famous fictional addresses, for it was here that Leopold Bloom, the central character in *Ulysses*, lived. You may have seen the original door of the house in the James Joyce Cultural Centre.

Rejoin Dorset Street. Directly ahead is the splendid spire of St George's Church [**58**]. Turn right and walk along Dorset Street. **Seán O'Casey** was born in number 85, on the right. A wall plaque identifies the location of the house, the site now occupied by a Bank of Ireland building.

*[Short optional diversion: Right of here, running parallel to Dorset Street, is Mountjoy Street. The poet **Austin Clarke** (1896-1974) lived between the years 1899 and 1910 at number 15.]*

Take the next left into Frederick Street North. The Joyce family lived at number 29 (demolished) Hardwicke Street, on the left, in early 1893. Number 4 is Waverly House, featured in **Joyce**'s short story, *The Boarding House*.

'*All the windows of the boarding house were open and the lace curtains ballooned gently towards the street beneath the raised sashes. The belfry of George's Church sent out constant peals, and worshippers, singly or in groups, traversed the little circus before the church, revealing their purpose by their self-contained demeanour no less than by the little volumes in their gloved hands.*'

From *The Boarding House*

Continue down Frederick Street North and turn right at Findlater's Church [**59**] into Parnell Square North. On your immediate right is number 18. Built around 1780 and restored by Dublin Tourism between 1989 and 1991, the house re-opened as the **Dublin Writers Museum** on 18 November 1991. It houses collections of rare editions, manuscript items and memorabilia relating to a long list of Irish writers, all in an eighteenth-century townhouse setting. There are also temporary exhibition rooms, a library of rare books, a gallery of portraits and busts, a bookshop and areas for lectures and readings. In adjoining number 19, the **Irish Writers Centre** offers a setting in which writers can meet, talk and work.

Retrace your steps to the corner and cross to the right and go down the hill, passing the **Garden of Remembrance** [**60**] on your right. The marvellous sculpture at the end of the garden is of the **Children of Lir** who in ancient Irish mythology were turned into swans for nine hundred years by their stepmother Aobh, or Aoife. The children spent three hundred years on Lough Derravaragh in Westmeath; three hundred years on the Strait of Moyle, between Ireland and Scotland; and three hundred years on the Atlantic by

Bronze statue of James Joyce

the islands of Erris and Inishglory. When Aoife's step-father Bodb Dearg discovered what she had done, he changed her into a demon of the air and no more was heard of her.

As you descend, look over at number 5, the birthplace of the poet, senator and surgeon **Oliver St John Gogarty** (1878-1957). Gogarty was a friend of James Joyce in the early 1900s and was the prototype of the character Buck Mulligan in the opening passage of *Ulysses*. Near the bottom of the hill on the right is the **Gate Theatre**, founded in 1928 by Hilton Edwards and Micheál MacLiammoir and renowned for its consistently high standards of stage design and performances. Orson Welles acted here when he was a young man, before he went on to make his name in Hollywood.

Walk the length of O'Connell Street along the central mall. Immediately after the Anna Livia Fountain, cross to the Café Kylemore to view the bronze statue of **James Joyce** by

Marjorie Fitzgibbon, at the top of North Earl Street. Joyce's head is inclined towards the General Post Office (GPO) [**19**]. The poet, writer and patriot **Patrick Pearse** led the Easter Rising occupation of this building in 1916 and proclaimed Ireland a republic from its entrance. He was executed on 3 May 1916.

Continue to the Larkin statue [**18**], opposite Clery's department store. Lines of Monaghan born poet **Patrick Kavanagh** are inscribed on the plinth, as are words of **Seán O'Casey**. At the end of the street, cross to the central island on the bridge and, when you reach the far side, go right at the fork onto the left side of Westmoreland Street. Stop outside Harrison's Restaurant. One of fourteen pavement plaques tracing the footsteps of Leopold Bloom in the eighth chapter of Joyce's *Ulysses* is on the pavement outside the restaurant.

*'Hot mockturtle vapour and steam of newbaked jampuffs rolypoly poured out from Harrison's.'*

At the end of Westmoreland Street, cross to the pedestrian island directly opposite the entrance to the House of Lords. An uninspiring bronze statue of **Thomas Moore** (1779-1852) hides behind some trees. Patrick Kavanagh wrote: 'The cowardice of Ireland is in his statue ...' in the opening line of his poem *A Wreath for Tom Moore's Statue*. Moore was a noted poet of his day and is today remembered for his earliest poems, *Irish Melodies*, which became known as *Moore's Melodies*. He was a friend of the patriot Robert Emmet, and later a friend of Lord Byron. He is commemorated here, beside Trinity College which he attended between 1795 and 1798.

James Joyce wrote satirically of the fact that Moore stood over the 'meeting of the waters', a reference both to the actual Meeting of the Waters in Avoca, Co. Wicklow, immortalised in song by Moore, and to the meeting of the waters of Dublin's citizens in the public urinal which is situated underneath the statue. Another Ulysses pavement plaque reveals all:

*'He crossed under Tommy Moore's roguish finger. They did right to put him over a urinal: meeting of the waters.'*

Cross to Trinity College front gates. Two statues by the celebrated sculptor John Henry Foley face onto College Green. The one on your left as you face the front arch is the philosopher and writer **Edmund Burke**. The other is the poet and playwright **Oliver Goldsmith**. Both attended the College in the 1740s but only became acquainted some years later in London. Here, both men have identical legs, which, I suppose, we must put down to a shortcut in sculptoring practice and not on a bizarre physiological coincidence.

Using your very own legs, go through the main arch and enter Front (Parliament) Square. This is the oldest part of the college [**52**].

Among the many graduates of Trinity who were later to become significant literary figures were **Samuel Beckett, Oscar Wilde, Jonathan Swift, John Millington Synge, Bram Stoker, Oliver Goldsmith, Edmund Burke, Thomas Moore, Joseph Sheridan le Fanu, Douglas Hyde, Oliver St John Gogarty, Percy French and Samuel Ferguson**. Contemporary figures include the poets Derek Mahon and Brendan Kennelly; novelists J.P. Dunleavy and William Trevor; and the essayist and political commentator, Conor Cruise O'Brien.

Of **Swift**'s time as a student, only the red-brick Rubrics buildings, past the Campanile, remain. They were built one year before he received his doctor's degree in 1701. **Goldsmith** spent his time here a penniless student, a monetary state of affairs which was to follow him through his life. **Oscar Wilde** [**114**] had rooms on the first floor of house number 18 in Botany Bay, a quadrangle (with tennis courts) behind the Graduates' Memorial Building on the east (left) side of Library Square (the one beyond the Campanile). To the right of the Campanile, on Library Square, is the **Old Library** [**52**] in which is housed the 1,200 year-old **Book of Kells** and other magnificent works of religious art of the period. The Library also houses the country's most important collection of original books and manuscripts. In the Long Room Library upstairs – a majestic sixty-four metres long room with a beautiful barrel-vaulted oak ceiling – 200,000 of the oldest books in Ireland are housed.

A fitting place to finish a literary tour.

At 707 hectares (1,752 acres), the Phoenix Park is Europe's largest enclosed urban park. It is larger than the combined acreage of Regent's Park, Hyde Park, Kensington Gardens, St James's Park, Green Park, Greenwich Park and Battersea Park – in other words, the area of all of London's main parks. The three-metre high boundary wall is eleven kilometres in length, with eight gates for vehicles and six for pedestrians. It has been managed by the Office of Public Works (OPW) since 1860 and was designated a National Historic Park in 1986.

You are about to embark on a leisurely stroll. Take time to absorb the sights, sounds and smells. Inside the park, the city seems a million miles away. Nature is unquestionably the star attraction.

**Tour begins:** *at the main entrance to the park, adjacent to Parkgate Street.*

Credit for the creation of the Phoenix Park as it largely exists today lies with the first Duke of Ormond and Lord Lieutenant of Ireland James Butler, who followed instruction given by King Charles 11 on 23 May 1663 '… to enclose or impark with a stone wall, in such a manner as you have already begun, such lands of our ancient inheritance or new purchase as you shall think fit for that use, and to store with deer.' The Duke carried out the King's instructions and stocked the park with fallow deer and partridge. In 1667 a wall was built to prevent deer poaching and to confine the herd. In 1747 the Lord Lieutenant, Earl of Chesterfield presented the park to the City of Dublin for use as a public park.

Enter the park along the right footpath, passing the attractive gate lodge, built in 1811, and walk up the main thoroughfare, Chesterfield Avenue. On your immediate left is an area of the park known as the **Klondike**, and closed to the public.

## Tour Facts

- **Length of tour:** approximately 6.5 miles (10.4 kilometres)
- **Duration of tour:** a brisk $2^1/_4$ hours, or a leisurely 3 hours
- **Refreshments:** during the tour (Fionn Uisce Restaurant in the Visitor Centre; Phoenix Park Tea Rooms); after the tour (Ryan's pub or the Ashling Hotel, both on Parkgate Street)
- **Getting to the Starting Point:** Buses from city centre 25, 25A, 26, 51, 51B, 66, 66A, 67, 67A – get off at Parkgate Street. Bus number 10 stops on adjacent Infirmary Road – five minute walk downhill to main entrance.
- **Special Note for Walkers:** Take your time, bring a picnic and a drink. If you begin the tour mid-morning, you might like to have a light lunch in the Visitor Centre, before continuing the walk in the afternoon. Finally, and importantly, it is best not to undertake the second half of the tour (from the Papal Cross) unaccompanied. There have been isolated incidents of muggings in the Park in recent years and it is best not to wander off into quiet places on your own.

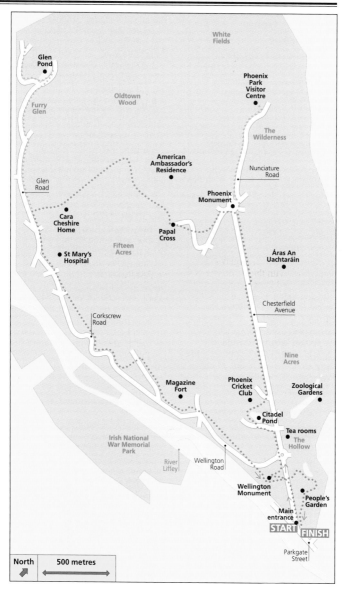

White Fields

Glen Pond

Furry Glen

Oldtown Wood

Phoenix Park Visitor Centre

The Wilderness

Glen Road

American Ambassador's Residence

Nunciature Road

Phoenix Monument

Cara Cheshire Home

Papal Cross

Fifteen Acres

St Mary's Hospital

Áras An Uachtaráin

Chesterfield Avenue

Corkscrew Road

Nine Acres

Magazine Fort

Phoenix Cricket Club

Zoological Gardens

Citadel Pond

Tea rooms

The Hollow

Irish National War Memorial Park

River Liffey

Wellington Road

Wellington Monument

People's Garden

Main entrance

**START** **FINISH**

Parkgate Street

North

500 metres

## Opening Times

- **Phoenix Park**
  Telephone: (01) 821 3021
  The park is open 24 hours a day
- **Phoenix Park Tea Rooms**
  Telephone: (01) 671 4431
  Mon–Fri 10am–3pm
  Saturday/Sunday/Holidays
  10am–6pm
- **Phoenix Park Visitor Centre**
  Telephone (01) 677 0095
  June–September  10am–6pm
  every day
  October  9.30am–5pm every day
  November–mid-March
  9.30am–4.30pm weekends only
  Mid-end of March 9.30am–5pm
  every day
  April and May  9.30am–5.30pm
  every day

The glasshouses here grow plants for the **People's Gardens**, an entrance to which is on your immediate right, thirty metres past the lodge. Visit these gardens at the end of the tour. Continue along the avenue for about 300 m until you reach the **Wellington Monument**. Cross to have a closer look.

The monument was built as a memorial to Arthur Wellesley, Duke of Wellington and, at almost sixty-three metres of Wicklow granite, is Ireland's tallest monument. Designed by Robert Smirke in 1817, it wasn't completed until 1861. Indeed, the committee overseeing its construction ran out of funds before the intended statue of Wellington on horseback was erected alongside the obelisk. Two of the friezes on the plinth depict scenes from the Duke's battles, in India and Waterloo. The lettering was provided from the metal of two small cannons captured in the Peninsula Wars. The wide and gently graded steps which run up to the main body of the plinth provide uncountable hours of enjoyment for boys and girls discovering the joy of running up and down the strangely shaped steps. If you visit here on a Sunday afternoon the odds are high that you will see children careering up and down the steps, and perhaps a few parents doing the same thing, in pursuit of their lost childhood. You may even see me, or my childhood ghost.

Stay on the 'Cycling Prohibited' path as you continue on your journey along the left side of the avenue. After about 300 m, look across the avenue to the attractive kiosk which houses the **Phoenix Park Tea Rooms**, perhaps a place to visit near the end of the tour. If you do find yourself at the tea rooms, look down the hill behind to the 'Hollow', with its mature and newly planted trees growing on the bank and with a Victorian bandstand at the bottom. In bygone days brass bands were a familiar sight and sound here on Sunday afternoons.

Continue along the main avenue for about a hundred metres to an intersection of pathways. At this point, across the avenue, is a road which leads to the entrance to the **Zoological Gardens**, better known as Dublin Zoo and one of the oldest zoological gardens in the world. The debate over whether urban zoos have a valid role to play in education and conservation or are simply outmoded and cruel institutions continues unabated in Ireland and, while the heat of the debate has cooled somewhat over recent years, it will simmer away in the background until the moral dilemma is resolved. I'm on the side of the animals, so you'll understand if I don't recommend a visit.

Go left along the curved path towards the cricket pavilion and go through the gate into the **Citadel Pond**, which is surrounded by a fence. Walk to the right, almost halfway around the pond, and go through the gate. You are now facing the **Phoenix Cricket Club**. A sign along the avenue's pedestrian pathway states that the club was founded in 1830 and is the oldest cricket club in the country. However, according to Trevor West, author of *The Bold Collegians*, Trinity College Cricket Club was founded in 1835, followed two years later by the Phoenix Cricket Club, and followed in 1845 by Leinster Cricket Club. Evidence, then, that you cannot believe everything you read on signs – or maybe in books!

Walk towards the perimeter fence of the cricket grounds and then rejoin the main path along the avenue. After a couple of hundred metres, look across the avenue to a large, grassy area. This is called the **Nine Acres** and is home to the Irish Polo Club. The players' pavilion is at the far side of the polo ground. As you proceed up Chesterfield Avenue, the Dublin Mountains will reveal themselves on the left horizon – on a clear day!

Chesterfield Avenue, named after the Earl of Chesterfield, is 2.6 miles (4.1 kilometres) long and is lined with three rows of trees on either side: horse chestnut, beech and lime. There are three wooded areas to the left along here – Pump Wood, The Black Wood and Sankey's Wood, the origins of the names being uncertain. Over twenty-eight per cent of the park is planted with trees. The main species are common or pedunculate oak, ash, beech, sycamore, birch, hawthorn and evergreen or holm oak. In smaller numbers are cedar, lawson cypress and larch. You may be interested to learn that the street lamps which line the avenue are lit by gas, a practice re-introduced in the year prior to Dublin's Millennium celebrations in 1988.

About half a kilometre beyond the Polo Grounds you will come upon **Áras an Uachtaráin**, the Irish President's home, beyond a narrow break in the trees on your right. Cross the avenue and walk to the line of trees to have a closer look. The fine house was designed by park ranger and amateur architect Nathaniel Clements and built in 1751. It was a modest, two-storey, red-brick house which was later extended, becoming the residence of the Lord Lieutenant in Ireland and officially called the Viceregal Lodge. Over the years, both the grounds and the house were added to and improved upon, so much so that, by 1816, the Viceregal demesne had expanded to 160 acres with a lake, ornamental trees and an abundance of oaks and elms. The large numbers of deer in the park coupled with the existence of a luxurious residence acted as a magnet for British monarchs who made regular visits to hunt. In 1922, following the establishment of the Irish Free State, the house

Phoenix Park Photo: Peter Zöller

became the residence of the Governor-General. Sixteen years later Áras an Uachtaráin welcomed the first Irish President, Dr Douglas Hyde, into its Georgian splendour. The house you see today is much altered from the original building. Some of this alteration was carried out by the celebrated architect Francis Johnston. It was he who decided to plaster over the brick façade, thus changing the appearance of the house from Georgian to Regency.

Near where you are standing, the infamous Phoenix Park Murders took place, on 6 May 1882. The leader of the Irish Home Rule Party, Charles Stewart Parnell [22] was – in an attempt to destroy his political career – a prime suspect in the horrific murder of the Chief Secretary in Ireland, Lord Frederick Cavendish, and his Under Secretary Thomas Henry Burke. It was later revealed that the brutal knifings were the work of a secret society called the Invincibles.

Stay on the right side of the avenue and continue until you reach the **Phoenix Monument** in the centre of the road, erected by Lord Chesterfield in 1747. Curiously, the name of the park does not derive from the mythical bird rising from the ashes but from a nearby body of water or well, now extinct, which was reputedly filled with 'healing' water. The Irish term was *fionn uisce* (clear water) and it is believed that the Vikings, having difficulty with the correct pronunciation, began the process of language change which eventually led to the term *phoenix*. So the story goes. On your immediate right is an elaborate entrance to Áras an Uachtaráin which is rarely used.

*[Optional diversion: If you wish to visit the **Phoenix Park Visitor Centre** – and perhaps indulge yourself with tea and scones in the restaurant – continue past the Phoenix Monument for a few metres and follow the signs to the Visitor Centre. The sixteenth-century castle is the oldest historic building in the Park. It was incorporated into the Under Secretary's Lodge, and this later became the Apostolic Nunciature. The castle was recently restored and converted into a visitor information centre and, if you have the time, is well worth a visit. If you are interested in trees, you will want to see the Park's tallest, a Sierra Nevada redwood which has so far grown to over thirty-one metres.]*

From the Phoenix Monument, follow Embassy Road, identifiable by the formidable entrance walls and gates to the official residence of the American Ambassador to Ireland. This residence was formerly the **Chief Secretary's Lodge and Demesne** and, before that, the residence of Colonel John Blacquiere, Bailiff of The Phoenix Park in 1774. It became the Chief Secretary's Lodge when the

Government acquired the house and sixty-acre domain in 1784 and housed the Chief Secretary here. It has been in official diplomatic use by the United States since 1927.

Continue past the Ambassador's residence and, after about 150 m, cut diagonally right, through the young trees, to the car park. In front of you is the **Papal Cross**, thirty-five metres tall and erected to commemorate the visit of Pope John Paul II, in September 1979. The Pope celebrated mass here in front of over one million people. Climb the mound on which the cross stands and survey all before you. The wide expanse of grassland in front of you is known as the **Fifteen Acres**, from an ancient and enclosed area of grassland. (Until 1984, the grasslands in the Park were grazed by cattle, however nowadays the grass is cut, baled and removed by a contractor.) The Fifteen Acres today covers about 200 acres. In times gone by, duels were fought here and military displays were held. Apart from the aforementioned Papal Mass in 1979, some other massive public events have taken place here, most notably the Eucharistic Congress in 1932 at which the gifted Irish tenor Count John McCormack sang.

From your vantage point on the Papal Cross mound you may see some of the Phoenix Park resident deer. There are four varieties of fallow deer in the park: Black, Brown, Common and Menil. About 500 live freely and unhindered and are usually to be found in the area of the Fifteen Acres and in the area of Oldtown Wood. Fallow deer originated in the Mediterranean region and were brought to Ireland by the Normans in the thirteenth century. Deer have lived in the park since 1662. At its peak the herd was about 1,300 in number while, at its lowest point, at the time of the 'Emergency' in Ireland during the Second World War, there were only forty in the herd.

From the Papal Cross walk right, keeping the boundary of the American Ambassador's residence at your side. Soon, the house comes into full view. After about 500 m, the boundary wall curves around to the right. This is the entrance to **Oldtown Wood**, one of the largest woods in the park and home to many oaks, hawthorns and ash. The Phoenix Park once had a far more extensive tree cover than at present, a good proportion of these being hawthorns. According to records, approximately 1,700 hawthorns were decimated in a ferocious storm on 27 February 1903. Altogether, 2,948 trees were blown down. Over 100 surviving hawthorns from that big wind stand resolute and firm in Oldtown Wood. In 1986 an extensive tree planting programme was undertaken throughout the park. Many were hawthorn woods and two of these were planted in Oldtown Wood.

Stand at the entrance to the wood and turn around to face the Dublin Mountains. Across the Fifteen Acres and nestled among trees is a large building, the Cara Cheshire Home. Walk across the Fifteen Acres, keeping the house on your left. When you reach the line of the house, continue right of the house for about 300 m, passing a lodge on your left named Knockmarry Lodge, built by

Decimus Burton in 1840. The lodge is beside an excavated Neolithic or early Bronze Age burial mound, the Knockmarry Burial Mound. In the 1838 excavation, a stone chamber was uncovered which contained the remains of two adult males and the bones of an animal, probably a dog. Also uncovered were small shells which formed a necklace. Drop down to **Glen Road**, straight ahead, a winding road which meanders inside the park's south-western boundary.

*[Thirty- to forty-minute diversion: Turn right and walk up Glen Road for a few hundred metres until you reach on your left a steep and narrow pathway running downhill to the wooded **Glen Pond**, a very popular area for walking at weekends. (A word of caution: because the path and the lake are quite secluded, it would perhaps be best to avoid this area unless you are accompanied.) You can, if you like, continue up the opposite side of the hill, along the pathway, until you reach the top and the **Knockmaroon Information Centre**. Five thousand years ago, Neolithic and Early Bronze Age Man were settled on a narrow strip of land between Knockmaroon and Islandbridge, further west. This land was strategically located, overlooking as it does the River Liffey. Burial sites which have been excavated in the area are older than the Boyne Valley passage graves of Newgrange, Dowth and Knowth. To rejoin the main tour, retrace your steps.]*

Go left along Glen Road towards the city. Take the left fork in the road a hundred metres

beyond the Cara Cheshire Home, signposted **St Mary's Hospital**. Both institutions provide long-term care and accommodation for the elderly. St Mary's was formerly the Royal Hibernian Military School, built in 1776.

The trees along here are home to grey squirrel, very common throughout the park despite the first sighting of its kind being as late as 1978 – in Áras an Uachtaráin. Red squirrels were once associated with the park, however the last recorded sighting of a red squirrel was on St Patrick's Day 1987. As you might imagine, the park is home to a wide variety of mammals, including badgers (almost exclusively to be found within the safety of secured residences, such as Áras an Uachtaráin and the Ambassador's residence), foxes, rabbits, stoats, bats, mink, otters, wood and field mice, pygmy shrews and brown rats. Wolves were once common, however they were persecuted and finally hunted to extinction in Ireland.

And let us not forget our feathered friends, the birds of the Phoenix Park. About sixty different species have been observed over a one-year period. These include, in the open parkland, jackdaw, rook, hooded crow, starling, mistle thrush, swift, swallow and goldfinch; in the woodland areas, blackbird, sparrowhawk, woodpigeon, robin, wren, blue tit, jay, owl, goldcrest and pheasant; and around the ponds and lakes, mallard, moorhen, coot, tufted duck, grey heron, mute swan and little grebe.

After several hundred metres, you will arrive at a crossroads – proceed in a straight line and climb to the brow of the hill on the left and walk parallel to Glen Road until you get to Corkscrew Road (easy to see where it gets its name). Drop down to the road and continue until the sharp bends in the road are left behind.

Go left away from the road along here, where you see the low, concrete building fifty metres in off the road. These are very basic changing facilities for the hundreds of amateur football players who use the adjoining playing fields. Turn right at the far side of the changing rooms and walk towards the extensive ruins of the **Magazine Fort** on Thomas's Hill. The fort was begun in 1735 and completed in 1801. On its completion, it was used as secure storage for ammunition and gunpowder, as well as serving as a barracks. The moat (still very much in evidence) and drawbridge provided considerable defence from possible attack. The fort had replaced Phoenix House, the manor house of the Phoenix Park and residence of the viceroys in Ireland from 1617.

Walk around the right of the fort. From this vantage point, you have a fine view across the Liffey to the War Memorial Park in the foreground and the south Dublin suburbs and Dublin Mountains. Look left into the city – can you identify the Royal Hospital Kilmainham tower, the spire of St Augustine and St John the Baptist church on Thomas Street, the Civic Office 'Bunkers' of Dublin Corporation on Wood Quay, the Central Bank on Dame Street, the copper-green dome of the Four Courts and, finally, Liberty Hall? Continue around the fort. When the Wellington Monument comes

into view, drop down to the road and climb the opposite hill and make directly for the monument.

Back at the Wellington Monument, if you have the time and the energy, cross Chesterfield Avenue and enter the **People's Gardens** through the narrow gate a little to the right of the monument. The gardens were laid out in 1864 by the Earl of Carlisle and comprise nine hectares of Victorian horticulture. The trees include silver birch, turkey oak, whitebeam and a tree of heaven. At the edge of the pond – at the far side – are weeping willow and weeping birch. Near the playground – to the right of the pond – ornamental maples were planted in recent years. The heavily wooded area is named the **Bishop's Wood**, after the Bishop of Limerick who lived for a time in Newtown Lodge in the Zoological Gardens. In 1841 naturalists Charles Gavan Duffy, John Blake Dillon and Thomas Davis met underneath an elm in this wood and decided to establish *The Nation* newspaper, which was to become an influential nationalist organ.

Leave the gardens by the gate nearest the main entrance to the park (this will be directly to your right as you entered the gardens from opposite the Wellington Monument). Near the exit, on the left, is a recently restored eighteenth-century building. It was designed by James Gandon as a military infirmary and is now the headquarters to the Irish Army.

To complete the tour, walk down into Parkgate Street and call in to Ryan's pub [**92**] or the Ashling Hotel for a post-tour refreshment.

*131*

The notion of a canal which would connect Dublin with the Shannon River and thus establish a waterway link between the east and west of the country was given serious consideration as far back as 1715. When the scheme eventually got under way in 1756, it was the beginning of a massive construction project which would last for almost fifty years and which would culminate, in 1805, in boat traffic travelling between James Street Harbour (beside the Guinness Brewery) and the River Shannon, a distance of 169 miles.

The route you are about to follow is along 2.5 miles (4 kilometres) of the banks of the Circular Line – 4.2 miles (6.7 kilometres) if you choose to do the long tour. Along the way are leafy and shaded towpaths, graceful lock gates, stone bridges and resident waterfowl.

**Long Tour begins:** *on George's Quay, opposite the Custom House and beside Tara Street Station.*

After admiring the Custom House [54] walk towards the sea, along George's Quay, City Quay and, finally, Sir John Rogerson's Quay. Directly across the street from the City Arts Centre and beside the Matt Talbot Memorial Bridge is a statue by James Power of **Matt Talbot**, a legendary Dublin figure about whom some lines are in order here, even though his story has nothing to do with the Grand Canal.

Talbot was born in Dublin in 1856 and, in his early teens, began to drink heavily and move from job to job. Sometime before he reached the age of thirty, he decided to take a pledge of total abstinence. He became a devout Catholic again, rising at four in the morning to prepare himself for daily mass. Around this time he began to live a life of extreme self-denial, sleeping on wooden

| Opening Times |
|---|
| • **Waterways Visitor Centre** |
| Telephone: (01) 677 7510 |
| <u>June–September</u> |
| Every day  9.30am–last tour 5.45pm |
| <u>October–May</u> |
| Wed–Sun  12.30pm–last tour 4.15pm |

planks and using wooden blocks as pillows. His food consisted of dried bread and cocoa, and he dispensed with his once inseparable pipe and tobacco – he had smoked an ounce of tobacco a day until then. From 1900 on, he worked in a large timber yard and developed the habit of giving away most of his earnings, a charitable practice he continued until his death. It was not until his death in 1925 that it was discovered he wore a heavy chain on his waist, a lighter one on his arm and a third below the knee cap on one leg. Yet, he was described as always cheerful and good humoured. In 1976 the

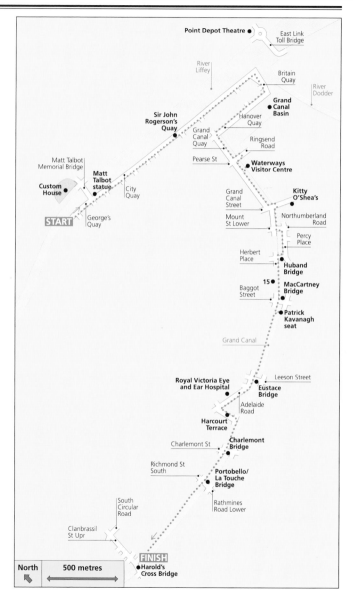

133

## Tour Facts

- **Length of tour:** 2.5 miles [4 kilometres] (the short tour); 4 miles [6.4 kilometres] (the long tour)
- **Duration of tour:** 1 hour (the short tour); 1 hour 40 minutes (the long tour)
- **Refreshments:** during the tour (any of the numerous restaurants, cafés and pubs on and around Upper Baggot Street; the Barge pub on Charlemont Bridge); at the end of the tour (nothing obvious in the immediate vicinity, I suggest you wait until you get back to the city centre)
- **Getting to the Starting Point for the short tour:** from the front gates of Trinity College (turn right and walk 300 m along College Street and cross to the Screen Cinema and catch a number 3 bus to the IDA Business Centre on Pearse Street. Walk from there to the bridge in front of you and turn right into Grand Canal Quay. The Waterways Visitor Centre is on the left. If you are feeling fit, you can easily walk from College Street along Pearse Street to the Visitor Centre, a twenty-minute walk); from any DART station (get off at Pearse Station, turn right along Westland Row and immediately right into Pearse Street. Walk for ten minutes and turn right into Grand Canal Quay. A new station at Barrow Street, on the far side of Grand Canal Basin, was due to open in 1999 but has run into planning difficulties)
- **Getting to the Starting Point for the long tour:** from O'Connell Bridge, walk down Burgh Quay until you reach Tara Street DART Station on George's Quay.
- **Special Note for Walkers:** sections of the long tour are along very quiet quays (you might find them a little too quiet and isolated) and between long, uninteresting warehouses. While I feel there is a great deal to see and enjoy on the longer tour, I have included a shorter tour as an option.

Catholic Church conferred on him the title 'Venerable'. He had previously been declared 'A Servant of God'.

Continue, passing the **Catholic Immaculate Heart of Mary Church** (1863) on City Quay and the **Seamans' Memorial** a little further on, erected to commemorate the thirteen Irish merchant ships and their crews lost in World War II. Further along, look at the keystone heads of the original Carlisle Bridge (now O'Connell), positioned on a red-brick warehouse adjoining Slattery's Office Supplies. Carlisle Bridge was replaced by the existing bridge in 1880.

**Sir John Rogerson's Quay** (1713), which runs the length of the quay from here, is named after the Chief Justice who was responsible for its construction. This entire area has been neglected for decades and is on the threshold of a major transformation. The Dublin Docks Development Authority (DDDA) is entrusted with the planning and implementation of a complete redevelopment of the

area from here to the end of the quay, and south as far as Pearse Street. Big business is moving in and there are fears that it could suffer the same fate as Temple Bar, i.e. total commercialisation.

At the end of Sir John Rogerson's Quay – when you cannot proceed any further – look across the Liffey to the **Point Depot Theatre**, one of the city's most popular live event venues in a converted Victorian railway shed. East of the 'Point' is Alexandra Basin, a busy shipping harbour. Turn right into Britain Quay (not marked) and walk to the three canal locks: Camden Lock, Buckingham Lock and Westmoreland Lock, all dating to 1796. This is where the Circular Line of the canal – the one you are about to walk along – joins the Liffey. It is a reasonable assumption to make that the majority of Dubliners have never been to this quiet spot. The River Dodder also joins the Liffey here, over to the left.

Look south and you can plainly see the Dublin Mountains – on a clear day, that is! Directly ahead is the **Grand Canal Basin**. Turn right and walk along Hanover Quay. After a couple of hundred metres, access to the edge of the water is blocked by warehouses, so continue your journey for a few hundred metres along Hanover Quay, but between uninteresting warehouses due for imminent demolition. At the end, turn left into Grand Canal Quay.

After 250 m, turn left and walk

The Liffey from Sir John Rogerson's Quay

**135**

to the hump of MacMahon Bridge and survey the Canal Basin on both sides. Cross the bridge – take extreme care, this is a busy street – and walk to the **Waterways Visitor Centre** (the unusual new building sitting out on the water).
**Short Tour begins:** *at the Waterways Visitor Centre.*

The visitor centre houses an exhibition which explores Ireland's inland waterways, their historical background and their modern amenity uses. If the centre is open, a visit is strongly recommended. The exhibitions are imaginatively presented and the information easy to absorb.

Directly opposite the visitor centre is the **Tower Design Craft Centre**, filled with small craft makers in a fine 1862 granite stone building. Turn left when you leave the visitor centre and walk along Grand Canal Quay. Go under the very low stone bridge above which run the DART, as well as mainline trains to Wexford and Rosslare. Turn left at the end of the street and walk the short distance to the hump of the canal bridge. *(For those on the long tour, a possible refreshment stop near here is Kitty O'Shea's pub, a popular watering hole a hundred metres beyond the bridge and on the right).* Carefully cross the street at the bridge and drop down to the canal's towpath on the right. Walk along this quiet stretch of the canal to the lovely stone bridge ahead. Northumberland Road runs off to the left from the bridge to the Victorian suburb of

Ballsbridge. The interesting red-brick building on the corner was formerly St Stephen's National School and is now a hotel. The road right, Lower Mount Street, leads to Merrion Square and the east end of Nassau Street.

Cross the bridge to the stone monument on the far side, with carved cross-guns and an inscription in Irish. It commemorates the violent skirmish which took place here during the 1916 Easter Rising when some Irish Volunteers positioned in adjoining houses caused mayhem among British Army soldiers heading to support their colleagues in other parts of the city.

Walk along the left bank of the canal, beside Percy Place. Admire the lovely terrace of residential houses on both sides of the canal along here. At the next bridge, **Huband Bridge**, built in 1791, look right to view the back of **St Stephen's Church** on Mount Street Crescent, commonly referred to as the Peppercannister Church [**104**]. Stand in the middle of the bridge and enjoy the tranquil and beautiful view east and west along the water and towpath. It is perhaps the loveliest urban view of the canal you will have.

The word canal is derived from the Latin *canalis*, meaning artificial waterway. The invention of the lock, attributed to the Chinese in the tenth century, made it possible to raise or lower vessels while afloat. Leonardo da Vinci invented the swinging – or mitre – lock gates which were used throughout the Irish waterway system.

Canals were an ingenious response to the transport problems of an era, problems which were mirrored across Europe, though which were particularly acute in Ireland. Road surfaces in the early-to-mid-1700s in Ireland were appalling. The knowledge that heavy goods could be moved more easily when floated on water was not lost on those who saw water as a solution to seemingly insoluble transport problems. On a road – even a reasonably good road – a horse drawing a wagon could move less than two tons on short journeys: on a canal, a single horse could pull a barge with a load weighing more than fifty tons.

When completed, the Grand Canal system covered, in total, 350 miles, including 123 on the River Shannon and 30 on the River Barrow. It served eighteen counties in addition to Dublin and left behind a remarkable engineering and architectural legacy – the cut-stone chambers of the locks, the massive wooden gates, the aqueducts, the cuttings, the embankments, bridges, tunnels, great basins, warehouses and hotels.

Amidst all this nostalgia, spare a thought for the lock-keepers of the lock gates. Their day was never done, with ten to fifteen boats passing through some of the Main Line locks on an average evening, on their way to different parts of the country.

Cross the bridge and continue along the right side, keeping on the towpath and not on the street pavement. The houses of Herbert Place are on your right. The Anglo-Irish novelist **Elizabeth Bowen** (1899-1973) was born at number 15. There is a wall plaque marking the house [**104**]. Ahead is **MacCartney Bridge** (1791), more commonly known as Baggot Street Bridge. Ascend the stone steps and walk to the centre of the bridge. Upper Baggot Street runs downhill to the left and is the beginning of the leafy and exclusive Victorian suburb of Ballsbridge. The red-brick corner house on the far side of the bridge is called Bridge House and was built in the year of the Easter Rising. The Monaghan-born poet **Patrick Kavanagh** spent much of his time in the building when it traded as a well-known bookshop, named Parsons.

Cross and continue along the right side of the canal, which offers tranquillity and shade in a busy district. Wilton Terrace runs parallel on your right. Between the two lock gates is a commemorative seat to the songwriter, artist and engineer **Percy French** (1854-1920). Cross the water by means of the narrow, wooden boards attached to the second lock gate and view the commemorative seat to **Patrick Kavanagh** [**103**], directly opposite Percy French's seat and erected by Kavanagh's friends on 17 March 1968, a year after his death. Beside the seat is a five-foot, three-sided, marble monument commemorating the

twinning of the Grand Canal with the Grand Union Canal in England in 1995.

Cross back to the other side and walk left for thirty metres to the bronze sculpture of a life-sized Kavanagh, seated on a bronze seat and sculpted by John Coll. Famous lines from the poet are inscribed on the pavement plaque beside the seat. Here are some others:

*'A swan goes by head low with many apologies,*

*Fantastic light looks through the eyes of bridges,*

*And look! A barge comes bringing from Athy,*

*And other far flung towns mythologies.'*

Join the poet on the seat for some quiet, reflective moments. It is not difficult to appreciate why Kavanagh loved this part of the canal which was in his time a quieter place. Nowadays, the passing traffic on the far side is an incessant intruder on this otherwise peaceful scene. The trees around here are full of character and the towpaths on both sides provide exquisite walks. At lunchtime on Mondays to Fridays, workers emerge from the countless offices in the vicinity, all seeking a more

Patrick Kavanagh

**138**

natural ambience than indoor lighting, central heating, ringing telephones and stressed-out bosses.

Continue to **Eustace Bridge**, built in 1791 and more commonly known as Leeson Street Bridge. Look right, down Leeson Street to the trees of St Stephen's Green in the distance. A journey left will bring you around by the Burlington Hotel and, further on, to Donnybrook village. *[The Burlington Hotel is a possible refreshment stop, five minutes walk from here, or the old traditional bar of O'Brien's pub, 200 m from here, in the same direction.]*

You now leave the banks of the canal for five minutes. Cross and turn right, towards Leeson Street, then *immediately* left into Adelaide Road. As you proceed along this shaded road you will pass on your left after 150 m the Dublin Hebrew Congregation building and, across the street, the impressive **Royal Victoria Eye and Ear Hospital**, built in 1897. Despite the recent closure of many of the city's older hospitals and their incorporation into large, modern institutions in the suburbs, this particular hospital is to keep its entire operations (!) on Adelaide Road for the foreseeable future. Beyond the hospital, on your left, is **St Finian's Lutheran Church**.

Turn left into **Harcourt Terrace**, built around 1840 and the only remaining Regency terrace in Dublin (only the houses on the right). The co-founders of the Gate Theatre, Hilton Edwards and Micheál MacLiammoir, lived in number 4. In the corner house at the canal end, the artist Sarah Purser lived from 1887 to 1909.

Rejoin the canal here and turn right and proceed to **Charlemont Bridge**. A left turn at the bridge will bring you to the busy village of Ranelagh. Cross and continue along the right towpath, passing the Barge Bar and Lounge (*possible refreshment – or lunch – stop*) as you go. Across to the left is a line of attractive terraced houses, set back from the busy road – if you can see them through the weeping willow trees beside you. At the end of the terrace there is a fine view of the copper-green dome of the Catholic **Mary Immaculate Refuge of Sinners** church, designed by Patrick Byrne and built in 1854. The dome stands out in Dublin's skyline and can be picked out easily from almost any vantage point on the Dublin Mountains. Ahead is **Portobello** (or, **La Touche**) **Bridge**, built in 1791. From the bridge, look left along Rathmines Road towards the bustling village of Rathmines. The red sandstone tower in the distance is **Rathmines Town Hall**, designed by Sir Thomas Drew and built between 1897 and 1899.

Cross to Portobello House, the large building on the right, facing the canal. It was built in 1807 as the **Grand Canal Hotel**, one of five hotels along the waterway at the time. The building later became an asylum for the blind and, later still, a hospital. It is now an educational institution.

The painter Jack B. Yeats spent his remaining years in the house, from 1950 until his death in 1957.

During Portobello's heyday the hotel was a busy place, situated as it was at the canal's passenger terminus. Passengers embarked and disembarked boats which carried about eighty people in first- and second-class cabins. On the boats, meals were served at tables between two rows of seats which ran the length of the cabin. Above the cabin was a flat roof encircled with railings and decked with seats – this area was for first-class passengers only. The mode of travel was slow – at speeds of three-to-four miles per hour – yet many travellers preferred the leisurely barges, where a decent meal could be enjoyed, to the speedier yet bumpy and sweaty stage coach journeys, where food was out of the question and there was always the lurking danger of robbery.

A canal boat traveller recorded the sixty-three mile journey between Dublin and Shannon as having been completed in a day, albeit a very long day, from four in the morning to ten in the evening, at a cost of twenty-one shillings for a first-class cabin, exclusive of entertainment, and fourteen shillings and one penny for a second-class ticket. In 1834 a narrower and lighter boat, the fly-boat, was introduced. It was pulled by four horses which proceeded at approximately nine miles per hour.

*The aforementioned stage coaches – giant carriages carrying up to thirty people on scheduled services – began with short journeys from Dublin in the 1730s. A hundred years later, the Italian-born Charles Bianconi, who had arrived penniless in Ireland and had travelled the length and breadth of the country as a boy selling religious pictures, had built up a horse-drawn coaching service that was affordable for the ordinary traveller and covered the entire country.*

The **Grand Canal Company** had a large fleet of horse-drawn barges on the Grand Canal. By 1924, the last of their boats had become motorised. These motorised boats were identifiable by the letter 'M' painted on the bow and the stern. Private companies or individuals who had their own boats and who used them to transport cargoes of wheat, maize, turf, coal, machinery and many other commodities were called bye-traders. Their boats were identified by the letter 'B' painted on the front.

The introduction of the railways to Ireland and their subsequent growth caused a corresponding decline in canal use. The last passenger boats were withdrawn in 1852. Trade boats continued, but with increasing competition from the railways and road freight, they too decreased in number, despite the fact that the Guinness Brewery continued to use the inland waterways to transport their brew right up to the middle of the 1900s. In 1960, the Grand Canal Company amalgamated with CIE, the national transport company and, in the same year, CIE withdrew the last of the trade boats (the old harbour of Portobello was filled in at the same time). In 1986 the Grand Canal and the Royal Canal were transferred to the Office of Public Works (OPW) to be managed and maintained as a public amenity.

Continue on your journey, staying on the right of the canal. The area to your right is a warren of Victorian artisan dwellings in a neighbourhood loosely called Portobello. Dublin's Portobello does not have the same ring to it as London's Portobello. In time this may change, as the area is becoming more and more trendy with each passing year and the prices of the modest two-storey houses are ascending accordingly.

At Lennox Place, 200 m along, a sign points to the right to the birthplace of **George Bernard Shaw**, on nearby Synge Street [**101**]. Another sign (after 150 m) points to the **Jewish Museum** nearby. A terrace of very low, single-storey dwellings line the road along here, about as small as you can get. Continue to **Harold's Cross Bridge**, built in 1933. A carving of the head of the patriot Robert Emmet, who was arrested near here, is mounted on the eastern section. A left turn will bring you to the suburbs of Harold's Cross and Terenure. Ahead and slightly to the right,

you can see the tower and some of the buildings of Griffith College, formerly Griffith Army Barracks.

*[The Circular Line of the canal continues for several more bridges, however the route is less interesting and this tour now branches off to the right and returns to the city centre. If you want to explore the canal further, continue along the left bank, up Parnell Road, for about five more bridges.]*

To return to the city centre, go right and walk half-a-mile down Clanbrassil Street to St Patrick's and Christ Church Cathedrals. There is a very interesting wall plaque on number 52, two hundred metres from the bridge, on the right. It states that Leopold Bloom (hero of James Joyce's *Ulysses*) was born in the house in May 1866. 'Citizen, husband, father, wanderer, reincarnation of Ulysses.' Joyce placed the newborn and fictitious Bloom in this actual house.

If you wish to avoid Clanbrassil Street – a wide and uninteresting thoroughfare – go right from the bridge and, at Leonard's Corner, the busy junction 300 m down, turn right and walk along South Circular Road. Take any of the roads to the left off South Circular and weave your way through the network of largely nineteenth-century terraced houses towards the city centre. The least strenuous option is to go right from the bridge and catch any bus at the other side of the road – all will be heading for the city centre.

Dublin is famous for its pubs and no guide book worth its salt would omit a section on them. However, it would be impossible to complete, say, a tour a fifteen or twenty pubs so, to make life easy for you, I have designed a series of six short tours. Each tour is based in a particular district of the city, and no tour features more than five pubs. Ideally, you should read all the tours before deciding on which one to take, but if this is too much to ask, consult the accompanying map and do the tour which is most convenient to you. As you might imagine, the choice of pubs is highly selective and, naturally enough, personal.

Finally, if you are interested in seeing more pubs, that will not be a problem: there are over 800 licenced premises in Dublin!

## TOUR 1:
## A STONE'S THROW FROM O'CONNELL BRIDGE
(Palace Bar; Zanzibar; The Flowing Tide; Mulligan's)

**Tour begins:** *at the Palace Bar on Fleet Street, around the corner from Bewley's Oriental Café on Westmoreland Street.*

Located at the doorstep to Temple Bar, **Palace Bar** is among Dublin's most famous 'literary' pubs. During the Irish Literary Revival in the 1930s and 1940s it was a popular meeting place for journalists and writers – you can see some interesting memorabilia on the walls recalling those times. The larger-than-life Irish Times Editor, R.M. Smyllie, resided in the back lounge most evenings from five o'clock and among his literary friends and acquaintances were the poets Patrick Kavanagh, Austin Clarke, John Betjeman and F.R. Higgins. The novelist Brian O'Nolan (better known by his pseudonym Flann O'Brien) and the playwright Brendan Behan

### Tour Facts
- **Length of tour:** all six tours cover a relatively small, localised area
- **Duration of tour:** this depends entirely on your mood – and your thirst
- **Refreshments:** you don't need me for this
- **Getting to the Starting Point:** see the beginning of each tour
- **Special Note for Walkers:** Never arrive at a pub, open the door, poke your head in, survey the surroundings, sniff the atmosphere and move off to the next pub. Not only is it discourteous to those inside, it misses the whole point of a pub tour, which is to soak up the atmosphere over a drink

were also frequent visitors.

The pub is structurally unchanged from those heady evenings of intellectual banter, but the clientele is more mixed now, the pub's literary history attracting a steady stream of tourists, while

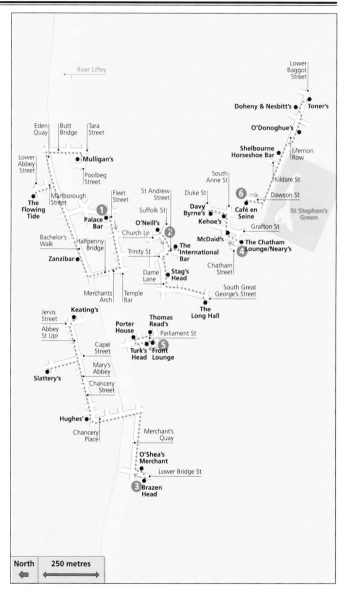

North    250 metres

the emergence of Temple Bar as a haven for nighttime revellers has brought a less discerning, more transient client, especially at weekends.

The front bar is long, narrow and solid and sub-divided by attractive partitions with inlaid mirrors. The bar is always busy. There is a neat little snug in the bar which you would barely notice (its door is usually closed). The back lounge is more like a living-room than a pub and there is a lovely quality of light which descends through the skylight during daylight hours. When seated – if you are lucky enough to find a seat – you can survey the comings and goings and listen – discreetly – to conversations nearby. If there are no seats free, patrons will usually not stay in this room but will retreat to the front bar.

Turn right when you leave the pub and walk along Fleet Street into Temple Bar. Although the origins of the district's name have absolutely nothing to do with pubs, you would be forgiven for assuming that Temple Bar is so named because of its concentration of pubs and nighttime revellers, such has been the unprecedented growth in the number of pubs here since the mid-1990s. Neither should you be fooled into believing that the pubs in Temple Bar are original and typical of the characteristic, old-style Dublin pub. They are not. In the blink of an eye – or, more aptly, in the swallow of a pint of porter – almost all the pubs here have been totally refurbished, many in fact having been torn asunder from the inside and rebuilt, leaving the original façade – and nothing else! – intact. Some years ago I would have recommended a visit to The Norseman and to Flannery's, both located on the central thoroughfare which cuts through Temple Bar. No longer: the two pubs have been so radically altered that their architectural heritage has been shattered.

Turn right when you get to Temple Bar Square and walk through Merchant's Arch and cross the Halfpenny Bridge to the north side of the river. Cross to the opposite pavement and go right, along Bachelor's Walk, until you get to **Zanzibar**, a pub as different to the three other pubs on this tour as is possible to be. It is very new, very modern, very trendy – and very young. In essence, it is one of the new breed of 'theme' pub. Now, your guess is as good as mine as to what the actual theme in Zanzibar may be. The name and some of the décor suggest a specific theme, but the entire place is so over the top that it really doesn't matter whether you are meant to be drinking in Zanzibar or Zagreb. This is where Dublin's youth pub culture thrives at the end of the millennium. The key words are: big, brash, loud – and it's all so incredibly popular. Enjoy your drink, if you can stand the chaos.

Continue along Bachelor's Walk when you leave Zanzibar – if you *can* leave Zanzibar! – and, when you get to O'Connell Bridge, continue in a straight line across O'Connell Street and along Eden Quay. (You might be surprised to learn that there are no pubs of note on the city's principal thoroughfare.) Turn left into Marlborough Street and walk to the next corner. The Abbey Theatre [**118**] is to your right.

Diagonally across the junction is **The Flowing Tide**. Unsurprisingly, when the plays in the adjacent Abbey and Peacock Theatres are over, many of the actors and stagehands cross to wet their dry lips in this pub. The

Kehoe's

wood-panelled interior is covered in posters from both theatres and are a fascinating record of some of the great plays and performances over the years. Like most city-centre pubs, the clientele here – apart from the actors – is hard to define. Lots of people passing through, some regulars – in truth, a mixed bunch. The downstairs lounge usually has a younger crowd and is worth visiting to see more of those posters.

After wetting your lips in The Flowing Tide, retrace your steps to the corner of Marlborough Street and Eden Quay and turn left and walk as far as Liberty Hall, the high-rise office block on the corner. Cross back over the Liffey at this bridge. At the far side, continue in a straight line along Tara Street and take the first right into Poolbeg Street. On the right is **Mulligan's**. Dating from 1850, it is one of Dublin's most famous pubs and long believed to serve the best pint of Guinness in the metropolis. In truth, many pubs

can serve just as good a pint, but in the old days Mulligan's creamy pint was, by common consent, the classic pint. The pub's façade is a fine example of a traditional, Victorian pub front. Inside, the atmosphere is lively, often noisy, sometimes chaotic. There is always movement, people coming and going, never a dull moment. The pub's heyday passed when the nearby Theatre Royal was demolished in 1962. It received a more recent blow when the Press newspaper group, which had its offices and printing rooms beside the pub, went into receivership in the mid-1990s, removing at a stroke its nearest and most reliable clientele. The late U.S. President John F. Kennedy visited the pub in the mid-forties while he was working with Hearst Newspapers. The playwright Brendan Behan was a regular here, and the parlour at the back of the pub is featured in a scene from James Joyce's short story *Counterparts*.

*Your tour ends here. Safe home!*

## TOUR 2:
## FOUR OLD PUBS
**(O'Neill's; The International Bar; The Stag's Head; The Long Hall)**

**Tour begins:** *at O'Neills on the corner of Church Lane and Suffolk Street.*

*[From the Molly Malone statue at the corner of Grafton and Suffolk Streets, walk along Suffolk Street to O'Neill's. From the front gates of Trinity College, cross and walk along the left side of College Green and take the first turn left, up the narrow Church Lane. O'Neill's is on the left.]*

**O'Neill's** is one of the busiest – and noisiest – pubs in the city. Inside, there are five separate bars, one a glass-panelled cocktail bar. The Victorian mock-Tudor exterior is very attractive. The pub is built on the site of the Thingmote, the assembly place of the Viking administration. The mound on which the Vikings assembled was removed in the late 1600s to raise the level of nearby Nassau Street. The pub attracts a large number of staff from the adjacent financial and insurance institutions, as well as students and academics from Trinity College. In recent times the pub has become a popular meeting place for young drinkers and this trend is slowly but surely squeezing out the older clientele.

Leave the pub by the Suffolk Street exit and cross to the church (now the main tourist information centre in the city) and walk along St Andrew Street to **The International Bar**, on the corner of St Andrew Street and Wicklow Street. The mahogany interior, marble-topped counter, ornate glass windows and transient clientele combine to make this one of Dublin's more interesting places to have a drink. There has been a pub here for over 200 years, however the present building was built in the late 1800s. The upstairs lounge is frequently used for lunchtime theatre and for evening comedy. The pub is a popular haunt of rock musicians and writers.

When you've finished your drink, retrace your steps along St Andrew Street and turn left at the ENFO building into Trinity Street and left again, at the Bankers pub, into Dame Lane. Walk to **The Stag's Head**, founded by businessman George Tyson and designed by J.M. McGloughlin in 1894. With its original stained glass windows, a magnificent mahogany bar topped with red Connemara marble and sub-divided into stalls by finely executed partitions, and a backdrop of fine mirrors and beautiful brass lamps, the pub stands out as one of Dublin's most attractive Victorian bars, despite its rather ghoulish devotion to the severed heads of the magnificent stag. Not a pub for animal rights campaigners.

For your fourth pub, continue to the end of Dame Lane and turn left into South Great George's Street. On the right, after a couple of hundred metres, is **The Long Hall**, built in the 1880s. The pub's name comes from the long hallway along which female patrons would gather to drink. The pub has a unique interior, with a variety of crystal chandeliers, a beautifully decorated bar with antique glass and a fine pendulum clock. At the end of the bar is a dimly-lit back lounge, a nice place to take shade on a hot summer's day.

*Your tour ends here. Safe home!*

## TOUR 3:
## MUSIC WHILE YOU DRINK
**(The Brazen Head; The Merchant; Hughes; Slattery's; Keating's)**

**Tour begins:** *at the Brazen Head on Lower Bridge Street.*

*From O'Connell Bridge, walk west (upriver) along the southern (left) quays and turn left after less than half-a-mile, at O'Shea's Merchant pub, into Lower Bridge Street.*

**The Brazen Head** is across the street. The Brazen Head Hotel was established in 1666 on the site of a much older inn, said to exist here since 1198, but the present building dates from the early eighteenth century. Leading revolutionaries and nationalists met here during different key periods in Irish history, among them Robert Emmet, Wolfe Tone, Daniel O'Connell and Henry Grattan. Some of the leaders of the United Irishmen were arrested in the inn in 1797, the year before the '98 Rebellion. This is a pub you simply have to visit, though it does become ridiculously overcrowded during summer nights.

Across the street is **O'Shea's Merchant**, renowned for its live – and lively – traditional music. The pub is frequented in the main by people from rural Ireland who are living in Dublin or who are in Dublin for a day or two. In recent times it has become a popular watering hole for the more exotic visitor, the tourist (this is not to suggest that Irish countryfolk are not exotic in their own, inimitable way!). On most nights of the week O'Shea's is crowded and the live traditional music can, on occasion, be superb. There is a small wooden part of the floor at the end of the bar where traditional Irish set dancing is enjoyed on an impromptu basis. Take your chance and bring your dancing shoes!

When you leave The Merchant, turn right and retrace your steps along Merchant's Quay to the next bridge down river. The Four Courts [**63**] are on the opposite quay. Cross the bridge and walk along Chancery Place to the end. **Hughes** is facing you across the street, a little to your right. The music sessions here are impromptu ones and for this reason no guarantees are made that you will hear music at all. However, when the music is playing, it is generally of a high standard – as is the set dancing. One of the best free traditional music gigs in town, when you catch the right night. But then, life is a lottery, too!

Turn left when you leave Hughes' and walk several hundred metres to Capel Street. This is a quiet and dimly lit part of the city at night and you shouldn't walk along here unaccompanied. At Capel Street, turn left and walk the short distance to **Slattery's**, on the corner with Little Mary Street. The pub occupies the building in which the Gin Palace traded in the latter part of the nineteenth century.

Since the 1960s, Slattery's has been one of the mainstays on the live traditional gig circuit, although in more recent times a plethora of other venues have sprung up around the city, diminishing Slattery's once firmly held position as an important live venue. Many of the best-known names in Irish music today were regulars in Slattery's during its heyday, musicians such as Christy Moore, Paul Brady and Jimmy McCarthy. The downstairs bar has been modernised in recent times, but it manages to maintain a feeling of authenticity, behind the muted lighting. The pub is an 'early house', meaning you can visit here before – or after – your 8 a.m. full Irish breakfast!

When you leave Slattery's, retrace your steps down Capel Street and turn left into Abbey Street Upper and walk to **Keating's**, on the corner with Jervis Street. This was, until recently, a featureless pub in what seemed like the middle of nowhere, however an imaginative treatment of the interior has

Bruxelles

created an interesting and lively space. The pub is a popular meeting point and a venue for regular traditional music sessions.

*Your tour ends here. Safe home!*

## TOUR 4:
## AROUND GRAFTON STREET
(The Chatham Lounge; McDaid's; Kehoe's; Davy Byrne's)

**Tour begins:** *at the Chatham Lounge on Chatham Street.*

*[From the top (southern) end of Grafton Street, walk down the street and take the first left into Chatham Street. From the Molly Malone statue at the bottom (northern) end of Grafton Street, walk three-quarters the length of the street and turn right into Chatham Street.]*

**The Chatham Lounge** is better known to most Dubliners and to all its patrons as **Neary's**. It is a popular haunt of actors from the Gaiety Theatre on parallel South King Street. The stage door of the Gaiety and the back door of Nearys both back onto Tangier Lane, a narrow laneway running off Grafton Street. The pub's sober brick and limestone front, with its familiar pair of cast-iron arms and lanterns, is complemented by the plush atmosphere inside, with marble-topped bar, mahogany surrounds and brass lighting. The writer Brian O'Nolan (Flann O'Brien) was known to frequent the pub.

Go down the narrow street directly opposite Neary's to Harry Street, parallel with Chatham Street. **McDaid's**, on your right, is famous for the patronage it received in the 1940s and 1950s by three Irish writers, Brendan Behan [108] Brian O'Nolan [109] and Patrick Kavanagh [103]. It was renovated in the early 1990s and is always a busy, lively place and an essential visit for the Kavanagh, Behan and O'Nolan fans. The pub is unrecognisable from the rough and ready interior which attracted the three literary heavies (and heavy drinkers) and many other writers forty and fifty years ago. Across the street is Bruxelles, a Gothic revival building designed by J.J. O'Callaghan in 1890 and regarded as the architect's most successful pub.

After your literary drink in McDaid's, turn right and walk across Grafton Street to South Anne Street. Halfway along on the left is **Kehoe's**, the genuine article: a simple, traditional exterior and, inside, a wooden floor, finely-carved partitions sub-dividing the long bar, a cosy snug at one end and a small, intimate lounge at the other. Busy and uncomfortably crowded at times in the evenings, Kehoe's is a very pleasant place to be in outside popular drinking hours.

When it is time to leave, walk down the pedestrian lane beside the pub to Duke Street, parallel to South Anne Street. On your immediate left is **Davy Byrne's** [106], a popular watering hole for all and sundry. The republican revolutionary Michael Collins, Sinn Féin's Arthur Griffith, the playwright Brendan Behan, the novelist and short story writer Liam O'Flaherty and the painter William Orpen – all were known to drink here. Its greatest claim to fame, however, is its featuring in James Joyce's *Ulysses*, an event which is celebrated each year by legions of Joyce fans who travel from many countries to be in Dublin on Bloomsday, the fictional date in which the entire book is set. The name Bloomsday derives from the central character in *Ulysses*, Leopold Bloom. The 'action' of the novel takes place on 16 June 1904, the actual day that Joyce first walked out with Nora Barnacle in real life (Nora and James spent the rest of their lives together). In *Ulysses*, Bloom drops in to Davy Byrne's 'moral pub' at lunchtime and has a glass of burgundy and a gorgonzola cheese sandwich. The pub you see today bears little resemblance to the pub of Joyce's day. A conversion by the 'new' owners back in 1941 gave the premises a thorough going over. A feature of the pub are the strange and intriguing murals which decorate the walls.

*Your tour ends here. Safe home!*

## TOUR 5:
## AROUND TEMPLE BAR
**(The Front Lounge; The Turk's Head Chop House; The Porter House; Thomas Read's)**

**Tour begins:** *at the Front Lounge on Parliament Street.*

*[From Trinity front gates, walk along College Green and Dame Street. Turn right a hundred metres past the Olympia Theatre into Parliament Street. From O'Connell Bridge, walk west (upriver) along the south (left) quays to the next main bridge (not the footbridge) and turn left into Parliament Street.]*

Because all of the old pubs in Temple Bar have been 'upgraded and modernised', it seemed appropriate to ignore those pubs whose architectural heritage has been destroyed and instead choose four pubs which add to the contemporary flavour of the area. All four are on Parliament Street [**29**].

**The Front Lounge** is a modern classic. With its long lounge, furnished with plush settees and armchairs and dimly lit throughout, this is one of the coolest – as in hip – places in town in which to have a drink. The back section is conveniently called the **Back Lounge**.

**The Turk's Head Chop House** is certainly untypical in terms of Dublin pubs. Going by the interior décor, the extravagant bar and the external decorations, it is reasonable to assume that large sums of money were dispensed in the creation of this modernist watering hole. This is not a pub for the faint-hearted or those with claustrophobic tendencies, as it gets incredibly crowded late at night.

Across the road, **The Porter House** brews its own porter, ale and lager – and very palatable, too! The pub is a very recent addition to this area and one feels obliged to commend the courage of the proprietors in brewing their own in a city dominated by the brewery to beat all breweries, the big G. The interior design of the pub is also successful, the architect having created a variety of drinking spaces on several levels.

**Thomas Read's** is a fine, recent addition to the world of Dublin pubs. Its richly wooden interior and Parisian-style pillars, together with its large windows confidently looking across to the splendid City Hall, make this one of the city's best places in which to take a break from the stresses of city life. However, try drinking here on a Thursday, Friday or Saturday night and all those stresses will come flowing back.

*Your tour ends here. Safe home!*

### TOUR 6:
### AROUND THE SHELBOURNE HOTEL
**(Café en Seine; The Horseshoe Bar; O'Donoghue's; Doheny & Nesbitt's; Toner's)**

**Tour begins:** *at the Café en Seine on Dawson Street.*

*[Directly opposite the Mansion House]*

The **Café en Seine** is a new and lavish creation, more at home perhaps in Vienna than in Dublin. The extravagantly long bar and unusually high ceiling create a feeling of space when you walk in, a sensation which rapidly diminishes if you happen to stray in here on a busy night, for the space between the bar and the seating on the left is far too narrow, ensuring that a visit to the loo is a bladderingly painful experience. The best time to visit (the bar, not the loo) is in the morning time when you can have a coffee and brioche and admire the splendid interior in relative calm.

When you leave the Café en Seine turn right, walk to the top of Dawson Street and go left until you reach the Shelbourne Hotel.

Here, in the **Horseshoe Bar**, you can continue your observations of the well-heeled, trendy Dublin set. The hotel has long been a magnet for some of the city's upwardly mobile – and for those who like to watch them. On the literary side, Elizabeth Bowen, William Thackeray, Rudyard Kipling and George Moore are among the many writers who frequented the hotel over the years. You can also visit the newer bar which runs along the top of Kildare Street. When the Horseshoe Bar is overflowing, you can sometimes find a seat here.

Continue past the Shelbourne to Merrion Row, where one of Dublin's most famous pubs is located. **O'Donoghue's** is where the legendary ballad group, the Dubliners, began their formidable musical career almost forty years ago when they began banging out a few ballads to the pleasure of a packed house. Although these days the pub has become a popular tourist haven, it still remains an essential place to visit, if only to see just how many people can actually fit into a small Dublin pub if the body and spirit are willing. There are regular, impromptu traditional music sessions, day and night.

Further along the street, on the left, **Doheny & Nesbitt's** attracts members of the legal profession as well as media people and politicians from nearby Leinster House. It is one of Dublin's finest old pubs, with a magnificent antique front, a heavy mahogany bar counter sub-divided by fine, wooden partitions, and soft, unobtrusive lighting throughout. In recent times a lounge has been created upstairs and, even more recently, the back room has been upgraded and is now a very pleasant drinking space. However, it is the Victorian bar which marks this pub out as something quite special. Nesbitt's (the older generation refer to it as Doheny's) is a worldly-wise place and one gets the sense that the regular clientele have seen it all before – and maybe they have.

Beyond Doheny & Nesbitt's, on the other side of the street, is **Toner's**, a fine Victorian pub with a characteristic snug. The pub seems old and worn yet remains solidly resistant to what must at times be a strong temptation to follow the path of modernisation, a route many pubs have taken. Of particular interest are the old drawers which were once used for storing groceries and tea, and the pump handles of the old beer dispensers. This is the pub in which W.B. Yeats had his one and only drink in a Dublin pub. The story goes that poet and surgeon Oliver St John Gogarty, who lived in nearby Ely Place, brought Yeats here from his then home in number 82 Merrion Square. Yeats sat in the snug just inside the door and drank a sherry bought for him by Gogarty. When the sherry was drunk, the great man rose and said to Gogarty, 'I have seen a pub now, will you kindly take me home?' … so the story goes.

*Your tour ends here. Safe home!*
**This is the end of the series of tours of Dublin city pubs. May you stagger home carefully and wake up refreshed.**

# Bibliography

Bardon, Carol & Jonathan. If Ever You Go to Dublin Town – A historic guide to the city's street names. Blackstaff Press

Boylan, Henry. A Dictionary of Irish Biography. Gill & Macmillan

Brady, Shipman, Martin. Grand Canal Corridor Study. Department of Arts, Culture and the Gaeltacht

Broad, Ian & Rosney, Bride. Medieval Dublin, Two Historic Walks. O'Brien Press

Casey, Eamonn. The Dublin Pub Saunter. Pelican Marketing

Craig, Maurice. Dublin 1660–1860. Penguin

Curran, C.P. Dublin Decorative Plasterwork. London/Alec Tiranti/1967

Graby, John & O'Connor, Deirdre. Phaidon Architecture Guide Dublin. Phaidon Press

Igoe, Vivien. A Literary Guide to Dublin. Methuen

Healy, Elizabeth & Moriarty, Christopher & O'Flaherty, Gerard. The Book of the Liffey. Wolfhound Press

Joyce, James. Dubliners. Penguin

Joyce, James. Ulysses. Penguin

Lalor, Brian. Ultimate Dublin Guide. O'Brien Press

Liddy, Pat. Walking Dublin. New Holland

Lincoln, Colm. Dublin as a Work of Art. O'Brien Press

Maxwell, Nicholas. Digging up Dublin. O'Brien Press

McDonald, Frank. The Destruction of Dublin. Gill & Macmillan

McDonald, Frank. Saving the City. Tomar Publishing

MacLoughlin, Adrian. Guide to Historic Dublin. Gill & Macmillan

Miscellaneous contributors. The Grand Canal – Inchicore & Kilmainham. OPW.

Moriarty, Christopher. Exploring Dublin, Wildlife, Parks, Waterways. Wolfhound Press

Neary, Bernard. Dublin 7 – A Local History. Lenhar Publications

Nicholson, Robert. The Ulysses Guide. Methuen

Plunkett, Myles. This Is Dublin Pocket Guide. Gill & Macmillan

St John Joyce, Weston. The Neighbourhood of Dublin. Hughes & Hughes

Somerville-Large, Peter. Dublin. Granada

Wallace, Martin. Famous Irish Lives. Appletree Press

Wallace, Martin. 100 Irish Lives. Barnes & Noble Books

Walsh, Peter. Heritage of Dublin's Pubs. Guinness

Wyse Jackson, Patrick. The Building Stones of Dublin. Town House and Country House

# Index

# Index

# Index

# Index

# Index

# index